Th

Timberlake Wer
Court Theatre in 1985. Her plays include
Grace of Mary Traverse, *The Love of the Nightingale* and *Our Country's Good*, which won the Laurence Olivier Play of the Year Award in 1988. She has translated plays by Marivaux, Anouilh and Mnouchkine, and most recently Sophocles' *Oedipus Tyrannos*, *Oedipus at Colonus* and *Antigone* for the Royal Shakespeare Company. Her screenplays include *The Children* and *Do Not Disturb*.

Three Birds Alighting on a Field

TIMBERLAKE WERTENBAKER

faber and faber

LONDON · BOSTON

First published in 1992
by Faber and Faber Limited
3 Queen Square London WC1N 3AU

Photoset by Parker Typesetting Service Leicester
Printed in Great Britain by Clays Ltd St Ives plc

A CIP record for this book is available from the British Library

ISBN 0-571-16105-7

1 3 5 7 9 10 8 6 4 2

For Max

Three Birds Alighting on a Field was first performed at the Royal Court
Theatre, London, on 5 September 1991. The cast was as follows:

AUCTIONEER	Allan Corduner
BIDDY	Harriet Walter
ALEX	Patti Love
JEREMY	Robin Soans
JULIA	Shirin Taylor
NICOLA	Adie Allen
YOYO	David Bamber
LADY LELOUCHE	Mossie Smith
DAVID	Allan Corduner
MARIANNE	Patti Love
STEPHEN	Clive Russell
FIONA	Mossie Smith
SIR PHILIP	Robin Soans
GWEN	Adie Allen
ODYSSEUS	Robin Soans
NEOPTOLEMUS	Harriet Walter
JEAN	Adie Allen
CONSTANTIN	Allan Corduner
MR BOREMAN	David Bamber
MRS BOREMAN	Shirin Taylor
MR MERCER	Clive Russell
AHMET	Allan Corduner
PHILOCTETES	Clive Russell
RUSSET	Mossie Smith
PRIEST	Robin Soans
YOYO'S MOTHER	Shirin Taylor
CATHERINE	Adie Allen

Director	Max Stafford-Clark
Designer	Sally Jacobs
Lighting Designer	Rick Fisher
Sound	Bryan Bowen
Costume Supervisor	Jennifer Cook
Stage Manager	Neil O'Malley
Deputy Stage Manager	Katie Bligh
Voice Coach	Julia Wilson Dixon

Painting in Scene Nineteen by William Tillyer, courtesy of the Bernard Jacobson Gallery.

AUCTION

A well-dressed man standing on a podium next to a large canvas. The canvas is white.

AUCTIONEER: Lot 208, a painting by Theodore Quick, entitled *No Illusion*. As you can see: totally flat, authentically white. (*He looks at his audience and speaks very fast.*) I shall start this at eighty thousand pounds, eighty thousand, any advance? (*He looks.*)

Ninety thousand. One hundred thousand at the back. One hundred and twenty thousand, lady at the front. One hundred and fifty thousand. Any more?

One hundred and seventy thousand, two hundred thousand, two hundred and twenty thousand between the doors, two hundred and fifty thousand, two hundred and seventy thousand all over the place now.

Three hundred thousand at the back. Three hundred and twenty thousand, lady's bid now, at the very back, three hundred and fifty thousand, any more? Three hundred and seventy thousand between the doors. Madam?

Four hundred. Four twenty, four fifty, four seventy, five hundred at the back, at the very back, yes, five hundred and twenty thousand. Five fifty, lady on my left. Five hundred and seventy thousand on the telephone. Six hundred thousand all over the place again.

Six hundred and twenty thousand, six hundred and fifty, six hundred and seventy, seven hundred, seven twenty, seven fifty at the back. Seven seventy on the telephone again. It's against you all in the room at seven seventy, seven hundred and seventy thousand.

Eight hundred thousand, eight hundred and twenty thousand, a new bidder, and now at the back, almost in the street, eight hundred and fifty thousand. Are you still in, madam? Eight hundred and seventy thousand, eight hundred and seventy thousand, nine hundred thousand at

I

the back, nine hundred and twenty thousand, lady on my left, nine hundred and fifty thousand on the phone. Going on? No. Any more?

At the side, nine hundred and seventy, nine hundred and seventy thousand at the side, last chance àt nine hundred and seventy thousand, are you going on, madam? Selling at nine hundred and séventy thousand pounds, all done? One million on the telephone.

(*A gasp.*)

One million one hundred thousand at the side, in the aisle, any more? One million two hundred thousand at the back, selling at one million two hundred thousand, all done at one million two hundred thousand pounds, one million two hundred thousand pounds: it's yours, madam.

And now Lot 209, an illuminated billboard by Laura Hellish which you can see at the back, between the doors. We can't turn on its lights but they are pink and they say: ART IS SEXY, ART IS MONEY, ART IS MONEY-SEXY, ART IS MONEY-SEXY-SOCIAL-CLIMBING-FANTASTIC, which I believe is a quote from the director of a great national museum across the water. Thirty thousand starts this. Gentleman at the back, thank you.

Act One

BIDDY: I didn't at first understand what was happening. For someone like me, who was used to being tolerated, it came as a surprise. You see, before, everything I said was passed over. Well, smiled at, but the conversation would continue elsewhere. I was like the final touches of a well-decorated house. It gives pleasure, but you don't notice it. England still had women who went to good schools, and looked after large homes in the country, horses, dogs, children, that sort of thing, that was my voice. Tony – that's my first husband – said he found my conversation comforting background noise when he read the papers.

But then, silences began to greet everything I said. Heavy silences. I thought there was something wrong. Then I noticed they were waiting for more words, and these words had suddenly taken on a tremendous importance. But I was still saying the same things. You know, about shopping at Harrods, and trains being slow, and good avocados being hard to come by, and cleaning ladies even harder. And then, I understood.

You see, I had become tremendously rich. Not myself, but my husband, my second husband. And when you're that rich, nothing you do is trivial. If I took an hour telling a group of people how I had looked for and not found a good pair of gardening gloves, if I went into every detail of the weeks I had spent on this search, the phone bills I had run up, the catalogues I had returned, they were absolutely riveted. Riveted.

Because it seemed everything I did, now that I was so tremendously rich because of my second husband, mattered. Mattered tremendously. I hadn't expected this, because you see, my husband was foreign, Greek actually, and I found that not – well, not quite properly English, you know, to be

3

married to a Greek – after all, Biddy *Andreas*? I could
imagine my headmistress – we had a Greek girl at Benenden,
we all turned down invitations to her island – and Yoyo –
that's my husband, George, Giorgos, actually – he didn't
even go to school here – but he was so rich and I became used
to it – him, and me: being important.

SCENE TWO: BARE KNUCKLE

The Gallery. ALEX BRENDEL, *American, thirty-five and dressed in
labelled power clothes, is storming around.* JEREMY BERTRAND
stands still, watching her with fatigue. JULIA ROBERTS, *an elegant
Asian woman, mediates. And there is* NICOLA, *the girl at the desk.*

ALEX: Nobody wants this stuff any more.

JEREMY: These are some of the best works –

ALEX: My ass. White, flat, zipped, unzipped, everybody's bored
with it, bored. And this! Nobody ever took this seriously.

JEREMY: You're talking about the most interesting living –

ALEX: Yesterday's news, Jeremy. Tomorrow, fallout. You
couldn't even unload this on an arms dealer.

JULIA: We've unloaded worse.

ALEX: Yesterday.

JULIA: We have three museums interested.

ALEX: Anybody signed a cheque?

JEREMY: This isn't a shop.

ALEX: Yeah, that's the problem. You shoulda got rid of this stuff
a long time ago.

JEREMY: I worked very hard to get some of these. What I don't
understand is why suddenly no one seems to –

ALEX: It's going bad. I mean, it's burning, it's burning so fast
your gallery could catch fire.

JULIA: We have a Japanese –

ALEX: They want flowers. I don't see any flowers.

JEREMY: Number six.

(ALEX *looks at number six on the wall.*)

ALEX: Yeah? It's like the others. Nothing.

JULIA: The title: *Where there are no flowers.*

4

(*A pause.*)
We believe the Japanese want that one. They're moving into colour.

ALEX: The cheque?

JEREMY: Really, Alex, he's bought from us before. It's a corporation.

ALEX: Do you know what's happening in Japan right now?

JEREMY: I consider myself generally well informed. I read *The Times*, I watch the nine o'clock news.

JULIA: We're rather wrapped up in a by-election, Alex.

ALEX: Japan's going down the tubes. I have it from *Le Monde*.

JEREMY: Alex, *Le Monde*. French – only they could call their national newspaper 'The World'.

ALEX: It's time to look at the facts, Jeremy.

JEREMY: I didn't know there were facts in art. Dates perhaps –

ALEX: OK, Jeremy, you want dates, I'll give you two dates: December 3. December 12. If Liz Taylor can't sell a Van Gogh and a dead Warhol can't sell himself, something's wrong.

JEREMY: I know something's wrong, Alex.

ALEX: This is next for the bonfire, that's all. This stuff is New York. And this is neo-New York. New York is finished. Mary Boone is in trouble. Castelli's showing Old Masters. Basically, New York is closing down. My company was too late to save New York, but we can save England. Do you want to save England or don't you? Well, if you want to save England, forget about the Japanese. They're looking bad.

JEREMY: I thought they were invisible, that was the charm.

ALEX: I could've given them some advice, but they didn't ask me. Now what you've gotta do is get rid of New York.

JEREMY: I remember the American shows at the Tate, we were dazzled. The scale, the daring. Rothko's colours.

ALEX: They're looking old. You wanna look old?

JEREMY: The confidence, the freedom. The English avant-garde were painting loos.

ALEX: Where are those bathroom paintings?

JEREMY: Sorry?

JULIA: The Kitchen Sink.

JEREMY: Ah. Mm. Across the street, I'm afraid. I don't think they're doing too well with them.

ALEX: OK. Forget the bathrooms. This is England, right?

JEREMY: I think so. Well, it was.

ALEX: What do you think of when you think of England?

JEREMY: Soft voices. Accents, the sort of accents people used to have – or acquire.

ALEX: No, I mean when you think of your childhood.

JULIA: Jeremy grew up in Egypt, Alex.

ALEX: Oh, I'm sorry. I mean, am I supposed to be sorry? Does it mean something? In code, you know, in English.

JEREMY: No, no, Alex, it means I grew up in Egypt. Julia grew up in England.

ALEX: And what do you remember?

JULIA: Accents, yes, that's right.

ALEX: Well, maybe you two should be running BBC Radio Three and not an art gallery.

JEREMY: No, my brother's doing that: they're in even more trouble than we are. But go on, Alex, what is it you want to say? You can be American about it, we won't mind.

ALEX: I'm saying: England.

JULIA: You mean we ought to go national rather than international?

ALEX: You start that way, then you make it international.

JEREMY: That's not so easy.

ALEX: That's what I'm here for. England: tea and English muffins.

JEREMY: I think you mean crumpets.

JULIA: Stubbs fetched some very good prices last month.

ALEX: Cricket. Nah, forget the cricket. Croquet.

JEREMY: What am I supposed to do, frame illustrations from *Alice in Wonderland*?

ALEX: English gardens. The countryside. Yeah, Constable, Samuel Palmer.

JEREMY: I'm having trouble with my overheads, I can't go around buying a lot of Constables. I couldn't even afford the drawings.

ALEX: I'm not saying Constable, I'm saying England, but as it looks now.

6

JEREMY: It doesn't look like anything now. It's mostly motorways.

ALEX: Come on, I walk around London. People have gardens. Big gardens. We don't have gardens in America, we have lawns. Or else you own a mountain. You need something to do with gardens. Landscapes.

JEREMY: Julia?

JULIA: The sculptors –

JEREMY: No, please, I can't have heaps of coal in here. It'll give me asthma. Chalk circles – no –

ALEX: Well, Jeremy, you'll have to go out there and find some English landscapes. Trees, a dark piece of water, a windmill, but new, now.

JEREMY: Our painters aren't taught to draw any more. They wouldn't risk themselves on a tree. It's very difficult to do a tree, Alex.

ALEX: It's very simple. Either close down like number eleven and fourteen or find a man who can paint trees.

JULIA: What about a woman?

ALEX: I think you want to attract the couples market. It's growing. Couples go in together, she's got the eye, he's got the money. They meet the painter, have him around to dinner. Now if it's a woman and she's young, the wife will be jealous, and if she's old he'll be put off. Stick with a man. Make him big. He can drink, but I can't have him smoke, OK? Put the woman in a group show. The school of new English landscape, no, the English Garden School, you'll think of something. Better, invite Morris, he'll think of something. I don't think he understands art, but he sure has a way with words.

JEREMY: Morris knows we don't love him.

ALEX: If he wanted to be loved, he wouldn't have become an art critic. OK, now, the spring is good, we'll put a lot of tulips, no, we'll be really English and have one daffodil in a glass, somewhere obvious, it'll look real subtle. Get this guy to do some really big paintings and some jewels, for this wall here. I can see it.

JEREMY: I don't think this painter exists.

7

ALEX: Well, make him. Send somebody to life class, I don't know.

JULIA: Let me think. He has to be alive?

ALEX: Yeah. For the moment. To give interviews.

JULIA: Stephen Ryle. He's from the North.

ALEX: The North, that's good. Spirituality. Snow. Yeah. People are getting tired of haystacks and olive trees, parched grass. It looks too much like the greenhouse effect.

JEREMY: I think Julia means Manchester, Alex, anyway Stephen'll never – he's so angry.

ALEX: Angry. I like that. That's real sexy. Constable with balls. He's not political is he? Good. Now I gotta have lunch at Claridge's, can you call me a taxi?

JULIA: It's down the street.

ALEX: I know where Claridge's is, Julia, you don't expect me to arrive at Claridge's on foot, do you, I mean, how can I tip the doorman if he doesn't open the door for me.

(ALEX *leaves with* JULIA. JEREMY *looks at his walls.* JULIA *comes back.*)

JEREMY: Must I pay five hundred pounds an hour to be abused by an ignorant woman?

JULIA: She worked miracles next door. Alex isn't ignorant, she's just American.

JEREMY: Julia, you must learn about Americans. There is nothing more elegant than an elegant American. But Alex . . . Her family must have come from Eastern Europe. By the way, I've never tipped the doorman at Claridge's. I've chatted with him when it's been raining.

JULIA: I'm sure that made him very happy, Jeremy. Shall I get in touch with Stephen?

JEREMY: I think I stopped paying him a retainer after I went to see him in the country. He was so rude. And out of touch. Trees. When everybody wanted photomontages of young men in black leather. What made you think of him?

JULIA: His wife and I were in a therapy group together.

JEREMY: Therapy, Julia. Isn't that against your religion?

JULIA: What religion, Jeremy?

The circle bar of an opera house. YOYO ANDREAS *is making a speech.
He is in his mid-forties and speaks with a slight accent.*

YOYO: . . . buildings, Pericles told the Athenians, to drive away
despondency. And he concluded with these words which will
be familiar to all of you: 'Mighty indeed are the marks and
monuments of our empire and future generations will
wonder at us as does the present age.'

This, my lords, ladies and gentlemen, is how the Giorgos
Andreas Company sees Britain as we turn to our ambitious
project on London's noble, arterial river, so loved and sung
by all the poets of Europe.

Monuments, however, are not empty shells. Pericles
boasted of the Athenian festivals; we boast of the festivals in
this august opera house. And just as my company seeks to
preserve the excellence of the past, but continue history, so it
is sponsoring not one, but two productions.

The Andreas Company therefore donates five hundred
thousand pounds to the revival of a classical opera and five
hundred thousand to the production of a new opera. And
now I have great pleasure in presenting this cheque for one
million pounds to our great opera house.
(*Applause. They shake hands, hold the pose, then*
LADY LELOUCHE *takes the cheque.*)

LADY LELOUCHE: Whenever I look at a businessman I think of
marriage.
(*Some polite titters.*)
I think, that is, of the marriage of business and art. It could
be one of the most successful marriages ever. What better
partnership than art – fine, delicate and often wayward –
looked after by powerful and hard-headed business. Yes, let
us wish this marriage long and lasting happiness. And now as
befits this happy occasion, we will celebrate with the
champagne generously provided by Mr Andreas's company.
It is excellent, I have tasted it. Several times.
(*Applause, titters.* DAVID *approaches* YOYO.)

9

DAVID: Very good speech, Yoyo, very good.

YOYO: Thank you, David. You must listen to so many –

DAVID: Where did you find that quote about monuments? Is it in the *Dictionary of Quotations*? I'm always looking for something to open board meetings, I've run out of Shakespeare. You can't say 'nothing will come of nothing' too many times.

YOYO: I remembered it from Thucydides. I wanted something from Churchill, but he didn't seem very interested in architecture. Odd for a man with such a sense of history.

DAVID: We English aren't city people like you lot. London is where you do your politics and your accounts, and then you go to the country. Of course I'm all for your flats over the water, but why should I want one when I can go and fish in my own river? Or, in my case, my neighbour's river.

YOYO: You must see the flats, David. They will be – poetic – they will live in the landscape.

DAVID: Yes, well, I'll have a look. I suppose they're frightfully expensive.

YOYO: Early buyers will have excellent terms. And friends.

DAVID: Lady Lelouche, excellent speech.

LADY LELOUCHE: I hope some of these art people got my word of warning. We can't have too much waste and irresponsibility any more. Loved your Pericles, Mr Andreas, suited you very well. Now we must do something for you . . .

YOYO: Thank you, Lady Lelouche, what I would love most would be the Royal Box for the Handel first night. Perhaps you would join my wife and me for dinner, and you too, David.

LADY LELOUCHE: Ah, yes, well. The Royal Box.
(*She drifts off.*)

DAVID: You should have asked me for the box, Yoyo. I'm off to the club, I'm going to ask for that Thucydides, how do you spell it? I suppose the librarian will know. Any other books with good quotes? Something from the Romans? I never get a chance to read. I've just agreed to the Tate – at least the art world understands business, can't say that about the theatres I deal with. So, yes, something Roman . . . You might even become a member, that way you could order the books, save me remembering how to spell them. Yes, you might enjoy that, nice club, famous architect, I forget his name.

YOYO: Ah yes, Sir Charles Barry.

DAVID: Well done with the million, Yoyo, hope they don't waste it on something too modern. You can always state a preference for tunes, you know. Don't let them intimidate you with all this artistic independence nonsense. You paid the money, you call the tune.

SCENE FOUR: INTERIORS

Glyndebourne, the gardens. YOYO *and* BIDDY *sit, in full evening dress, shivering with cold, and look apprehensively at the sky. Sounds of voices and the popping of champagne corks.* BIDDY *lays out an elaborate meal on a table cloth: champagne glasses, silverware, etc.*

YOYO: It was going well. After all he'd suggested it two months ago and I had been very careful not to seem eager, but I thought I would casually drop it into the conversation and he began to ask me about my interior life. I thought it was one of those English expressions, but I couldn't ask, so I mentioned that film I love, *Interiors*, and finally he came to the point and asked me if I liked walking in the Lake District, but said I probably wrote poetry, most Greeks did, and was I keen on hunting? Tell me, Biddy, what does hunting have to do with an interior life?

BIDDY: Grooming the horses at dawn, the chase, it's thrilling –

YOYO: (*Over her*) Isn't that Richard Bede? What is he doing at Glyndebourne, he only owns a restaurant. Then I thought, well, I have an English wife and surely she must have an interior life. Henry's wife writes biographies, he's always boasting about how he never reads them. That's what David meant, I'm sure. (*Looks around.*) We should have gone to the restaurant, everyone's there.

BIDDY: Last time you thought only the corporate people went to the restaurant. You wanted a hamper.

YOYO: And Jamie complains about all the concerts Caroline drags

him to and how difficult it is to talk to contemporary
composers – and so, darling, I'm waiting.

BIDDY: For what, Yoyo?

(*A short pause.*)

YOYO: An interest.

BIDDY: I'm interested in making you comfortable. Happy.

(YOYO *is cold.*)

And in the house.

YOYO: Why doesn't it look more English?

BIDDY: It did, Yoyo, before you asked me to throw out my
grandmother's things.

YOYO: All that chipped china and knives that didn't cut.

BIDDY: Yes, well.

YOYO: And those sofas.

BIDDY: I know they were hideous, but that's English, ugly pieces
of furniture one inherits from one's grandmother.

YOYO: Biddy, this hamper, didn't you used to have that for the
cat?

BIDDY: Yes . . .

YOYO: Biddy, surely we can afford to buy a new one.

BIDDY: Why? I'm rather attached to it. Mummy used an old
knitting basket for Aldeburgh.

YOYO: Aldeburgh – should we be going to Aldeburgh? What
happened to the furniture you had when you were married to
Tony?

BIDDY: Oh Yoyo, I couldn't ask for that. Not after that frightful
girl . . . No.

YOYO: I will not wait another year for the Progress. David could
forget. I've just given the opera house all that money, and
I'm in the press. I don't care what it is, Biddy, and how
much it costs, if you want to write something, we'll publish it
ourselves.

BIDDY: I hate writing letters, Yoyo. We could have horses, but
you don't like the country that much.

YOYO: It has to be better than that, better than all their wives.

BIDDY: Are you sure they're that interested in what their wives
do?

YOYO: Why else do they talk about them?

BIDDY: To make conversation, like the weather.

YOYO: I think you're allowing yourself to be out of touch, Biddy.

BIDDY: I'm sorry.

YOYO: There's Lady Soames. She's seen us. No, she's looking the other way. We've chosen the wrong part of the garden, no one's even walking this way.

    Ah, there's Lady Lelouche and David. Now do be interesting with her, she's everywhere.

BIDDY: Daddy loathes her.

    (LADY LELOUCHE *comes on with* DAVID.)

YOYO: Biddy! Lady Lelouche, do come and join us.

LADY LELOUCHE: Grass looks wet. It'll rain for Wimbledon. I had something urgent to say to you, Mr Andreas, what was it, something about Royal, Royal – Royal Garden Party? No. We've lost our guest, tall, went to look at a flower, you haven't seen him? Christopher.

YOYO: You know my wife?

LADY LELOUCHE: Ah, I remember now. Yes, the Royal Box. Impossible for the Handel, one of the directors wants it, but you can have it for the new thing, next season, what is it called, David?

DAVID: Can't remember, but you'll like it, Yoyo, it's about medieval England, kind of *Camelot* for the intellectuals, I think.

YOYO: Thank you, and you'll join us for dinner?

LADY LELOUCHE: Alas, we have some Texans that week.

DAVID: I never go to the modern stuff, Yoyo, if I can help it. I've spotted Christopher, Lady Lelouche, he's about to fall into a rose.

    (*They hurry off.*)

YOYO: Biddy, you didn't say a word. Why aren't we invited to the Royal Garden Party?

BIDDY: They're so dreadful. Even Daddy hates them.

YOYO: Couldn't he have given us his invitation?

BIDDY: Darling, it doesn't work like that. I don't know how it works, but not like that . . .

YOYO: Now listen, David invited me to lunch at the Progress next week. He will introduce me to one of the older members.

Then everything could go through quite smoothly. I want you to come.

BIDDY: Are you sure?

YOYO: And when you come, I want you to bring it up in the conversation.

BIDDY: What, Yoyo?

YOYO: You're being deliberately obtuse. Your interior life. And it had better be very interesting. I can't afford a wife who does nothing, Biddy.

(*A frozen silence.*)

We haven't talked to anybody. If we could get season tickets, we could invite people. Can't your father help?

BIDDY: The waiting list is fifteen years. He can't change that.

YOYO: Your father can't seem to do anything for us.

BIDDY: He did try with White's. Apparently the ones who are most against any change in the thing about the schools are all those Russian princes who, strictly speaking, shouldn't be there anyway. They certainly didn't go to school here, but they were irresistible in the twenties and one expected them to go back. But Daddy did say they were dying off, and if you could wait a few years, he'd try again.

YOYO: With another eight years on the waiting list? No, it'll have to be the Progress. I won't be happy until I sit in one of those large armchairs talking about Thackeray and smoking a pipe.

BIDDY: But, Yoyo, you don't smoke.

YOYO: Biddy, don't let me down. Biddy, it's over to you.

SCENE FIVE: WOMEN TALKING (WHEN WOMEN TALK THE
CONVERSATION IS ALWAYS ABOUT MEN)

JULIA: He actually threatened you?

BIDDY: He didn't wave the divorce papers in front of my face, but he – well, I remember it from Tony: he implied I was no longer suitable. In Tony's case it's because he had this girl half his age and he felt foolish, but Yoyo means it: I'm not helping – his ambitions. Julia, help me, I can't go through it again.

JULIA: Through what?

BIDDY: Everything: another divorce and then living alone,

shopping for pre-cooked meals for one at Marks and
Spencers.

JULIA: I cook for myself every night, I have fish, a delicious salad.
I listen to music, and over a demitasse of black coffee I read
an art journal. I have a great time.

BIDDY: And then the pub. That was in the country, but I would
sit there alone and the publican's wife would come and talk
to me because she felt so sorry for me. And when the
children came home for the weekend, when they weren't
spending them at Tony's, I couldn't remember how to talk
because I hadn't opened my mouth all week except to ask for
two apples.

JULIA: We had a good time in London.

BIDDY: You'd put on your sari and go visit your aunts for the
weekend, and I was afraid to go out in the street, I felt
everybody knew: rejected woman, alone. The silence, Julia.
I know Yoyo doesn't talk much and then he wants to spend
all his evenings at this club if only he can get in, but at least
he's there, the plumber knows he's there, the dustbinmen,
even if I have to deal with all that on my own, he's there, in
the background.

Julia. How can I become more interesting?

(*A silence.*)

JULIA: Come and work in the gallery.

BIDDY: You don't understand . . .

JULIA: I do. You're married to a creepy foreign social climber.

BIDDY: Julia! *You* can't –

JULIA: Why not? because I have foreign skin? I remember Yoyo.
Mind you, that's a miracle because I've hardly seen you since
you got married. You behaved like all married women and
immediately dropped your women friends, but never mind. I
remember him and I know the type.

My father wanted to be an English gentleman too. He
wanted to be an Englishman so badly he ended up an empty
shell: cashmere suits, his daughter at a convent school, an
English wife who recoiled from his dark skin.

Once we were in a taxi and the man was playing Indian
music and my father's head started swaying, then his whole

body and it was the first time ever I saw him alive, almost smiling, and then he shut the glass between us and the driver. And I have no heritage, I'm nothing. In India I'm a foreigner and in England, I'm an exotic. And the worst is that I've inherited his pretensions. I want to be a gentleman too, detached, elegant, self-sufficient, with a cashmere mind, but maybe I'm confused, maybe I really want to be a Buddhist, except I'm too angry to be a Buddhist. Too ambitious.

BIDDY: I remember your rages in the flat. You were so funny. Sometimes it was because you'd been out with an Englishman and sometimes because you'd been out with an Indian.

JULIA: No more. You were very sweet. Trying to understand racial confusion. Might as well have asked you to study quantum physics. I thought we had a good time, going to the cinema, to dinner, remember the holiday we had in Venice? I taught you to appreciate Giorgione.

BIDDY: I loved being in Venice with you, Julia, but –

JULIA: But it's not your identity. Your identity has to come from a man. Otherwise it's worthless. It's sick. Mind you, my identity comes from my boss, and I've just realized how stupid he is. I'm the Julia who works for Jeremy. Well, not for much longer.

(*Pause.*)

I know what Yoyo needs. He needs to become a collector. It's the passport to society in America and it's beginning to work here.

BIDDY: A collector? He likes stamps.

JULIA: Of contemporary art.

BIDDY: You mean Picasso? Isn't that a bit expensive, even for us?

JULIA: The Picassos of tomorrow, you fool, I happen to know who they are.

BIDDY: Oh. Who are they?

JULIA: It's not that simple. I'll have to guide you. You'll buy only what I tell you.

BIDDY: I see.

JULIA: If that's too much of an effort, why don't you just get a yacht?

16

BIDDY: Yoyo gets seasick.

JULIA: I thought they always came from shipping families. It'll have to be art then. You might even have fun.

(MARIANNE *approaches*.)

Just the person I want! Marianne, what a beautiful hat.

MARIANNE: I thought it might change my life. It didn't and now I can't pay for it.

JULIA: Why don't you send the bill to Stephen?

MARIANNE: Ha! He doesn't open his own bills.

JULIA: How is he these days? This is Biddy, also having some husband problems.

MARIANNE: I hope your husband is rich. Mine's a pauper. He shouldn't have been.

JULIA: Is he still doing landscapes?

MARIANNE: Can you believe it? He's studying all those war painters, you know, the ones who were sent out on their bicycles by Kenneth Clark to record England before the Germans invaded, and he's doing these comments he calls them – on their work.

And then some of his own, abstract. Who the hell is interested in the English landscape? I told him what people wanted now were grim depictions of urban blight or else just white, you know, everybody still likes white. Or even black, people respect black, it looks serious, like the Germans. Or you can do a little of everything: show you're confused. I do know something about art. He won't listen. I hate him. He hasn't recovered from the sixties. I bet he's still a socialist, secretly.

JULIA: I would like to go and talk to him. Biddy is a collector, she might come with me.

MARIANNE: Actually his stuff isn't that bad. It's his personality. These days it's not enough to have talent. Do you buy from Jeremy?

BIDDY: I'm just starting.

MARIANNE: Jeremy's very good. But it's really because of Julia.

JULIA: Do you have Stephen's number?

MARIANNE: He'll kill me if he knows I've given it to anyone. Here it is. I've just put myself down for the Tate Lectures.

(*To* BIDDY) I'll probably see you there. I had a fit last time when they said they were booked up. After all, my husband, well, my ex-husband, sold them some paintings. Of course no one remembers and they're rotting somewhere in their vaults. Everybody's at those lectures. I want to find a really nice pen to take notes with. Black, with some red, no, white and black . . . (*To* BIDDY) Get my husband to show you his early work. It was brilliant. Door handles. We had John Lennon at our show.

(*She drifts off.*)

JULIA: We were talking about art . . .

BIDDY: Yes, Yoyo . . . Yoyo has to get into the Progress Club.

SCENE SIX: UNTITLED

The Gallery. JEREMY, BIDDY *and* JULIA *are staring at a painting.* NICOLA *reads a magazine.*

JEREMY: Possibly his best.

(*All look.*)

It's extremely rare for something like this to come on the market. It's only because of the divorce. I heard she was in tears when he decided to sell it.

BIDDY: Who?

JEREMY: Charles, of course. Jane.

BIDDY: What was it, euh – Jane liked about it?

JEREMY: That there's nothing there.

(*Pause.*)

BIDDY: I see . . .

JEREMY: Julia spoke to her.

JULIA: She would be on the street and there was all this noise, cars, litter, mess, then she would come home and look at this. Columns and columns have been written about this painting. It's about America. I've got some of the articles at home, I'll let you read them.

JEREMY: But really, one need only look.

(BIDDY *looks.*)

This is irrelevant, but you might like to know his prices have gone up by four hundred per cent in two years.

BIDDY: My husband says the art market is rather depressed at the moment.

JEREMY: Good things never lose their value, Mrs Andreas, it's the second rate that's not selling. And I'm very pleased about that.

BIDDY: Have many people expressed an interest in this?

JEREMY: People don't call us, we call them. I'm very careful whom I associate with this gallery. I have two or three people I might offer it to, but I'd prefer it stayed in England. Will you open your collection to the public, Mrs Andreas?

BIDDY: Ah? Well, not immediately, I mean – I'll have to see . . .

JEREMY: I understand: a great collection is very personal. This is a difficult work, what we call a slow work. A great painting always is.

BIDDY: I find it, euh, very interesting, the, euh, emptiness, but, mm, could I take it home and try it with the house?

JEREMY: Alas, this isn't a carpet from Liberty's, Mrs Andreas, the insurance . . .

(BIDDY *walks towards and back from the painting.*)

BIDDY: I like it, I'm very interested, I just wondered, well – my husband tends to like things that are very English.

JEREMY: Why don't you bring him along? Did you tell me he was Greek? He'd like its Apollonian quality.

BIDDY: He's busy, he's left it to me, but, well, he'll want something English. You see, my husband loves Jane Austen . . . so . . .

JEREMY: I'm afraid only one English painter has reached international stature and you wouldn't like him, Mrs Andreas, believe me.

BIDDY: Do you mean Francis Bacon?

JULIA: Biddy!

BIDDY: I only know about him because I found two tickets to a show by him in Tony's pocket one day. I knew my first husband was having an affair because he was doing all these strange things like going to health farms and concerts and I went to the Francis Bacon to find out more about her.

JULIA: What did you find out?

BIDDY: Nothing, but . . . something about myself. Those men isolated – in their circles, so uncomfortable and smudged, well, I felt like that. It was so sad, but I left the exhibition feeling, I don't know, recognized, better. Do you have any of his paintings?

JEREMY: No. And he's hardly new, Mrs Andreas.

BIDDY: No, of course, well . . . I'm sorry.

JEREMY: Please . . . shall Nicola call you a taxi?

BIDDY: No, I'll walk, I need the fresh, I mean, I need some exercise, it's, it's –

JEREMY: Come to our next private view, Mrs Andreas.

BIDDY: Oh, yes, I'd love to – thank you.

JEREMY: It's a group show, but I may have one painting there . . . I believe I've discovered, well, rediscovered an unusual English painter, I'll let you in on his name –
(*Pause.*)

BIDDY: Stephen Ryle?

JEREMY: Who told you about him? Have you read something? He's mine! What I mean is that he shows exclusively with this gallery.

JULIA: I told Mrs Andreas about Stephen, Jeremy.
(JULIA *leads* BIDDY *out. A silence as* JEREMY *stares at the painting.*)

JEREMY: I can't sell it. (*To* NICOLA) Do you like it?
(NICOLA *nods, then shakes her head.*)
I read yesterday about an Italian clerk who had saved great Italian paintings from the Nazis. He knew exactly which ones to save, well, it wasn't difficult, he saved the Raphaels, the Leonardos . . . If we had an invasion here, what would I save? Would I save this painting? Would I save it because it is worth half a million, or was, yesterday, or would I save it because I was convinced humanity would be the poorer without it? *Would* humanity be the poorer without it?

SCENE SEVEN: THE ARTIST'S MODEL

Stephen's studio in the country. STEPHEN RYLE, *a big man of fifty, is lying very still. He is naked under a toga-like sheet which covers odd parts of his body and he wears a crown of leaves on his head. Standing not far from him is* FIONA CAMPBELL, *a woman of thirty. She is sketching quickly, looking mostly at his back, which is bare, and his profile. A long silence.*

STEPHEN: You won't get the curve of my back if you're so tentative.
   (*She ignores him. Another silence.*)
FIONA: Don't move.
   (*Pause.*)
STEPHEN: You're scratching that paper, not making love to it.
FIONA: I said, don't move.
STEPHEN: Assurance and speed. This is nature, it's a moment. You can fiddle all you want in the comfort of your studio.
FIONA: You've gained weight.
STEPHEN: Will it be my back or a generalized back? Do it again.
FIONA: No, Stephen, you can correct it later. If it needs it.
STEPHEN: All those years teaching you detail.
FIONA: I remember when I couldn't do a floor. You were so horrible. Paint the object, you shouted, then the shadow. The shadow'll make the floor.
STEPHEN: Well, now you can do floors. But can you do my back? Come and touch it. Make love to my back.
FIONA: You moved your head.
STEPHEN: Bring me your breasts . . .
FIONA: Stephen.
STEPHEN: I used to be able to draw them in two seconds, with my eyes closed. The breasts of a frontierswoman. Your awful father must have had a wonderful mother with wonderful American breasts, covered-wagon breasts, the breasts of the Wild West.
FIONA: She was from Boston.
STEPHEN: *Mayflower* breasts. Come here.
FIONA: I think we'll go to America after the show and look up some American relatives.
STEPHEN: I have an erection. Can you draw that?
FIONA: If you can hold it long enough. You didn't even notice I said We. Stephen: I've met someone. I'm getting married.

STEPHEN: What happened to that woman?

FIONA: That was just power. She modelled for me, I decided to seduce her. I'd like to be faithful. A new experience. I've treated men like restaurants. You were my favourite, but I liked to try the food in the others. I'd like some stability. I know that sounds Victorian.

STEPHEN: No, worse: New Age. You're having your first show in a glitzy gallery. Isn't that enough? You don't want babies as well, do you?

FIONA: Why not? You did.

STEPHEN: It's not the same. Fiona, you won't paint. I'll have wasted my time.

FIONA: I'm not Marianne. I'll never stop painting. You can't talk.

STEPHEN: I keep working.

FIONA: And don't show it. You rile against the market place like some effete modern composer.

STEPHEN: Fiona, the market place dumped me ten years ago.

FIONA: Please come to my show.

STEPHEN: I don't go to London. Is he an aromatherapist?

FIONA: Who?

STEPHEN: A medium? A social worker? No, even you wouldn't fuck a social worker. But, of course, you're getting married, you don't have to fuck him.

FIONA: Shut up. I warned Jeremy you'd be there. I'm your prize pupil. You don't have to talk to anyone.

STEPHEN: I had a letter from Jeremy the other day. How was I? He still had the door handles on his sitting-room wall, wouldn't sell it. Was I doing anything new? Could he see it?

FIONA: Aren't you?

STEPHEN: I showed him some work five years ago, my best. What does it mean? he said. I told him it wasn't a piece of conceptual art, it didn't need a book to go with it. What could I tell my clients, he said, why should they buy a landscape in 1985? Couldn't you do some more door handles? He could charge anything for those now. Then he asked me if I'd ever thought of making paintings that looked upside down, he said it could be a breakthrough for me. I threw him out. I told him he should be selling cars.

FIONA: Don't move. Maybe he's coming around.

STEPHEN: Fuck him.

FIONA: You can't hide your landscapes for ever.

STEPHEN: I see them.

FIONA: You taught us art was public.

STEPHEN: The world has changed. The public doesn't deserve art.

FIONA: Maybe it's changing again. I can make it change. You can. I will make it change. Everyone will be there. Please don't be rude and drunk.

STEPHEN: I'm not your husband, Fiona, I get drunk when I please. Does he like your work?

FIONA: He's not that visual. He has other qualities.

STEPHEN: Like what? He's kind to animals?

(*Pause.*)

FIONA: I'm finished.

(STEPHEN *gets up, stiffly, messily draping the cloth around him.*)

STEPHEN: I'm sure you've made it too elaborate. You always do. Let me see.

(*He looks, carefully. A long silence.*)

You've made me look old.

FIONA: I drew what I saw. You taught me not to flatter. I sketched you the way Velázquez would.

STEPHEN: It's not sensual enough. You don't love my skin. When Degas drew his old tired washing women, their skin was still sensual.

FIONA: That's not what it's about.

STEPHEN: It's a nude, isn't it? What's it called?

FIONA: Philoctetes. He was a great Greek warrior who sailed for Troy. But he was bitten by a snake and the wound wouldn't heal, causing him inexorable anguish. It also festered, so that he began to stink. His friends couldn't stand his smell any more, so Odysseus tricked him to an island where he was abandoned, with only a cave for shelter and berries for food. And his festering sore. Ten years on, the Greeks were told in a prophecy they could only win the war if he came back to

them with his bow and arrows, which made him invincible. So
Odysseus went to the island to try and trick him back to Troy.
STEPHEN: What happened?
FIONA: It's a long story.

SCENE EIGHT: 'POOR LAYMAN I, FOR SACRED RITES
UNFIT...'

The Progress Club. YOYO *and* BIDDY *stand waiting, awkward.*
DAVID *comes to them.*

DAVID: George. Good. Philip's still struggling with the Roof
Committee, we have more leaks every time it rains and we're
running out of buckets. You've brought your wife, how
charming. We're very progressive here, Mrs Andreas, we
actually have a women's division, about four I think, my
favourite is a charming old bird with a patch. We like to
continue our liberal traditions. Will you join us for lunch?
YOYO: Yes...
BIDDY: No... I don't think –
DAVID: And there's Philip. Philip, Mr Andreas and his wife. Mrs
Andreas – Sir Philip Morton, who single-handedly is trying to
stem the tide of decay sweeping over us – oh dear, I believe I'm
mixing my metaphors. Are you literary, Mrs Andreas?
(*A silence.*)
BIDDY: This is a beautiful room.
SIR PHILIP: Isn't it. And it changes remarkably with the light,
Mrs Andreas.
DAVID: Yes, we take it for granted, don't we, we're such
philistines.
YOYO: My wife is very interested in the arts.
DAVID: How charming. Charming. The arts. What would we do
without the arts? Pity they're so expensive.
BIDDY: (*To* SIR PHILIP) I've heard my uncle talk about this
hall...
SIR PHILIP: I don't want to bore you with a guided tour, Mrs
Andreas, but if you look, you will notice the frieze above the
columns. It was completed in 1841 by Sir Charles Barry and

24

is widely considered his masterpiece.

DAVID: Philip, I never knew all that. But why do we have so many leaks? Isn't it funny, George, Philip says this is the most beautiful building in London, but we're a ragbag of a club and we can't repair the roof.

SIR PHILIP: Don't say that, David, or Mr Andreas will defect to White's.

(*They all laugh.*)

YOYO: My wife's father was a member of White's.

BIDDY: He said he only went there for the puddings. It reminded him of school.

SIR PHILIP: Ah, yes. Treacle tart with custard. Bread-and-butter pudding.

DAVID: Do you know, the other day I had a bread-and-butter pudding made with brown bread, and I, who never complain, lost control of myself. The French chef came out and told me it was healthier. Mind your *onions*, I said, I remembered that bit of French from school, and leave bread-and-butter pudding to the English. Speaking of which, we'd better get into the dining room before the old codgers take best tables. Are you joining us, Mrs Andreas?

(YOYO *nods.*)

BIDDY: No, I'm afraid I have things to do.

SIR PHILIP: Quite right. My wife won't step into this place, says it reminds her of our son's gymnasium. She goes to Fortnum's and has a frightfully good time.

YOYO: Biddy . . .

BIDDY: I must go look at a painting. The exhibition closes tomorrow . . .

YOYO: Biddy's very interested in art. We're starting a collection.

DAVID: How charming. All that modern, blank stuff? Is it still blank? No, I read somewhere it's upside down now, German and upside down. Mm.

BIDDY: The painter I'm looking at is English. It's full of colour.

SIR PHILIP: English? Do we paint? I know we write. And we garden. I didn't know we painted. We used to . . .

BIDDY: Yes, we have a great tradition of landscape painting and it seems to be reviving. Of couse, it's different . . .

25

SIR PHILIP: We used to do so many things. We used to know how to repair roofs, make windows . . . I called a builder to my house the other day about some windows. He tried to convince me to replace my leaded windows with aluminium ones. More practical, he said. I do try to keep in touch, Mrs Andreas, I go to the odd private view. It all looks like aluminium windows.

BIDDY: You would like this, Sir Philip, it has that care.

DAVID: I hate anything abstract. Reminds me of algebra.

BIDDY: It's a language that can be learned. But these paintings are landscapes. And you recognize England in them. Of course, there's a lot of controversy, some people say this is parochial, we should like the upside-down paintings. I disagree. But do please excuse me, you see why I must look at these paintings again. I'll let you enjoy your lunch in peace.

(She goes. A silence.)

DAVID: Charming.

SIR PHILIP: They're so clever, women these days, aren't they, so . . . convinced. I understand why one might want to get away occasionally. Now, Mr Andreas, perhaps you can give me some advice. I'm on the Politics Committee.

DAVID: Philip, I thought you were going on to the Dining Committee.

SIR PHILIP: That would have been much more interesting, David, but I'm afraid they insisted they need me on this politics thing. It seems the Club want to shed some of our insularity, have better communication with Europe, particularly countries we've never thought of before, Spain, Greece, Turkey . . .

YOYO: I would be loath to call Turkey a European country, Sir Philip.

SIR PHILIP: Ah? You must know, tell me about it.

DAVID: Why do we have to worry about Europe, Philip, what's wrong with England?

SIR PHILIP: That's what the Europeans will tell us.

DAVID: What do they know? They're European.

SIR PHILIP: Now, you were saying, Turkey is not . . .

DAVID: You can't ask him, Philip, he's one of us now.

26

SIR PHILIP: Yes, but who are we?

SCENE NINE: THE ARTIST AND HIS FAMILY

Stephen's garden. GWEN, *eighteen, is weeding, vaguely.* STEPHEN *is mowing the lawn.*

GWEN: What I've thought is first I'd fly to New York and spend a few weeks, and then I'd go up to New England and watch their leaves, what's it called, the Fall, then I'd go to Canada and meet Robert and we'd take that train that goes across the mountains and – is this a weed, well, I'm pulling it out anyway – then we'd go to Alaska –

STEPHEN: How are you going to live?

GWEN: I thought you'd pay for some of it, and then I'd work, waitress or look after children in Canada, they have children there, don't they?

(*A silence.*)

Can you pay for some of it?

(*A silence.*)

I'm going to be a very limited person if I don't see the world.

STEPHEN: There are lots of things to see in England.

GWEN: Oh, Daddy, Devon, the Lake District, BORING – Sheep. Then Australia, I want to study the Aborigines, New Zealand, Antarctica . . .

STEPHEN: There are lots of sheep in New Zealand.

GWEN: Yeah, but they're not the same, they'll look different, I'm sure, they'll be more – well, they won't be English sheep. And then I could find a world cruise and work as a chamber maid back to England. Or maybe I'll stay in Australia, will you miss me? Or maybe I could stop in Morocco and take a camel across the desert like in *The Sheltering Sky* –

STEPHEN: As in –

GWEN: As in. Daddy, you're such a pedant. I'm going to need a camera to record all those travels, I thought if I had one now, I could practise so I learned to take brilliant pictures, as in Lord Snowdon. I saw some really good secondhand cameras in a shop and I could even take a course . . .

27

STEPHEN: How much?

GWEN: You could come and help me choose, Daddy, that would be fun. About two hundred. Maybe more for a good one. Will you come?

STEPHEN: Not to London.

GWEN: Why not? Why won't you ever come to London?

STEPHEN: It's my Troy.

GWEN: Troy? What's a Troy?

STEPHEN: It's a place where the Greeks and the Trojans fought. What did they teach you in that expensive school of yours, Gwen? And by the way, when are you going to retake? You must go to university.

GWEN: Daddy . . . maybe I don't really want to study, maybe I'm stupid, I don't know . . .

STEPHEN: You would have done better in a comprehensive instead of what's really no more than a finishing school.

GWEN: Daddy . . . don't start. I might become a great photographer. Will you buy me the camera? Oops, here comes Mummy. I suppose you two are going to have an argument, I'm going to sunbathe.

(MARIANNE *comes in. A silence.*)

MARIANNE: What are you planting now?

STEPHEN: An avenue of horse chestnuts.

MARIANNE: How long do they take to grow?

STEPHEN: Fifty years.

MARIANNE: What's the point?

(*A silence.*)

I need some money.

STEPHEN: You know I don't have it.

MARIANNE: What happened to that illustration work?

STEPHEN: I did three books last year. A *Guide to Breeding Gloster Canaries*, *Castle's List of Grasshoppers of the World*, I've blocked out the third, and when the editor rang me to tell me the crest of the canaries should look more like woks and less like frying pans, I swore I'd never do another one. Japanese carp, yes, that was the other one. I'm a painter.

MARIANNE: I have a friend who wants a portrait done of her and her husband.

28

STEPHEN: No.

MARIANNE: You're completely irresponsible. You have children, a wife.

STEPHEN: Ex-wife.

MARIANNE: You're still responsible for me.

(*Pause.*)

I wish I'd never married you.

STEPHEN: You didn't think so at the time.

MARIANNE: That's cheap. You seemed so promising in those days. That show of yours at the Serpentine. I knew you'd be impossible, but I didn't mind, I thought I'd be helping a great artist. I should've kept on painting myself. I gave it up to help you. All I wanted was to be an artist's wife. What a joke.

STEPHEN: I never stopped being an artist.

MARIANNE: I'm not so sure.

STEPHEN: (*Dangerous*) What do you mean?

MARIANNE: This going back to nature stuff. It was all right in the sixties, but to do it in the nineties. It's perverse. I don't think a real artist is perverse, I think a real artist reflects the times.

STEPHEN: What times?

MARIANNE: You could learn something in London. You stick yourself up in the country like some sour hermit, nobody lives in the country any more, you should see other people's work. You might learn something. I don't know why I even bother. The trouble with you is you don't know how to listen, and you have no values.

STEPHEN: And you do? You call money a value?

MARIANNE: It's a hell of a lot better than trees, isn't it? I could've married Richard. He's a millionaire by now. He hasn't compromised, he's just been a little more polite than you and more in touch. Well. I've always backed the wrong horse. I had feminist friends in those days, they told me I was crazy to get married at all, they were right. Now they've got great careers and I'm just, I'm just stuck here doing nothing, in a tiny London flat and it's your bloody fault.

STEPHEN: I never recommended London.

MARIANNE: Oh shut up, you know what I mean. And the girls.

Gwen has to beg you for a secondhand camera. It's pathetic. Camille doesn't even bother any more, I don't blame her. And you don't even care.

STEPHEN: Look, Marianne, I paid for those awful public schools you sent those girls to, and now I want to work. I happen to believe in what I'm doing.

MARIANNE: Yes, well –

STEPHEN: I'm not interested in art taken from the art magazines, I'm interested in this, these shapes, this energy around us . . . why don't you look? Try to feel something? Forget about money for five minutes.

MARIANNE: I have bills to pay, Stephen. I don't throw them in the fire the way you did before those bailiffs came when you stopped teaching at the Slade. It's all very well for you to look at me with contempt, and treat me like a nag, but I don't have a studio to escape to. I devoted my life to you, and now I have nothing to show for it. Nothing. Nothing. Nothing.

(*Pause.*)

STEPHEN: You have two very good-looking and spoiled daughters.

MARIANNE: They're growing up. They're getting competitive. I bore them.

STEPHEN: What happened to that counselling job? I sent you money so you could train.

MARIANNE: It was a dead end. The salary was pathetic.

I gave such great parties when you were starting out. I thought I could do something in that line, for young artists, but they get famous so quickly these days, they don't need me. And they're mostly twenty-five-year-old girls anyway. I'm not needed. I have no worth.

STEPHEN: I'm sorry.

MARIANNE: That's not good enough.

(*Short pause.*)

I made all the wrong choices. I hear your mistress is in Jeremy's new show. *And* getting married. Serves you right. By the way, Jeremy's asked after you. Look, if he asks to see something of yours don't be your usual rude self. Richard's been talking about nature, and he's always sensed the fashion, that's why he's so rich. I have a feeling you may be given a second chance. Don't spoil it.

I should've got married again. But successful men want blonde bimbos. And I couldn't marry another failure. Where's Gwen?

GWEN: I'm here, I've been listening. I'm remembering it all in case I become a writer. I'm never getting married. I'm going to support myself with photography but, Daddy, you'll have to buy me a camera.

SCENE TEN: PHILOCTETES, PART ONE

A Greek beach. ODYSSEUS (JEREMY), NEOPTOLEMUS (BIDDY).

ODYSSEUS: If Philoctetes sees me, he'll kill us both. I'm the one who left him on this island. Well, I had to. The wound never healed and his cries and moans drove us mad. And seeing that blood and pus. Also, he stank.

NEOPTOLEMUS: What had happened?

ODYSSEUS: Bitten by a snake. On the leg. Terrible poison. He was a great hero, before that, but there you are. Bad fate.

You must go to Philoctetes alone, convince him you're as bitter and angry with the Greeks as he is, that you've also been hard done by the world and by me. Flatter him, get him drunk if you can and steal that bow and the arrows. Then ask him to come with you. And if he won't, we'll make him.

NEOPTOLEMUS: I hate lying.

ODYSSEUS: We all do when we're young. But: if you don't lie, you'll die and if you don't lie very well, Greece will be finished. Since it's our duty to win that war and since we can't win the war without him and his bow and arrows, it follows that it's our duty to use whatever means we can to get hold of him. They call me Odysseus the Logician.

NEOPTOLEMUS: I thought it was the Wily.

ODYSSEUS: That's a mistranslation.

NEOPTOLEMUS: Isn't it wrong to lie?
ODYSSEUS: Right, wrong: shifting words in a shifty world.
NEOPTOLEMUS: I see him. Dragging his leg. So much pain on his face.
ODYSSEUS: I'll tell you a secret. No one likes to be lonely. Whatever they say.

SCENE ELEVEN: PRIVATE VIEW

The Gallery. A tray of wine and small bits of cheese. JEREMY *and* JULIA *stand, waiting.*

JEREMY: I forgot the daffodil.
JULIA: I thought of something better and ordered wild flowers. They're coming from Ireland, they'll be here later.
JEREMY: Can I afford wild flowers?
JULIA: No. Worry about Fiona. Her fiancé couldn't come tonight because he leads a trauma group every Tuesday. Read in that his work in group therapy is much more important than anything she does.
JEREMY: Doesn't Fiona qualify for trauma therapy? It's her first show.
JULIA: Fiona's furious and she's drinking.
JEREMY: Women are so unattractive when they drink. Perhaps everyone's right, they don't have what it takes to be successful artists.
    (FIONA *approaches and overhears.*)
FIONA: I heard that, Jeremy. That's a shitty thing to say.
JULIA: It's a slightly old-fashioned concept, that's all, Fiona. We'll change it.
FIONA: I have what it takes.
    (MARIANNE *comes in.*)
MARIANNE: I seem to be early. Or is no one coming? Where are your artists?
JEREMY: Germany, New York . . . You know Fiona.
MARIANNE: (*Looking around*) Bit of a ragbag, Jeremy. I can't tell whether you're going for the International or the English. Or

are you trying both out? Fiona's are good.

FIONA: Do you know my future husband said he was worried my paintings might be celebrating cruelty to animals. Because I put a fucking Greek myth on a canvas. What he's going to fucking do, censor Greek myths to save the Green party? Where's Stephen?

MARIANNE: He won't set foot in these places, you know that.

FIONA: He said he'd come.

JEREMY: Did he? Marianne, you must talk to him.

MARIANNE: Fiona can do it better than me. (*To* FIONA) I'm sorry you've split up. It's the only thing that made him still attractive to me, the fact that you loved him. He must have some value, I thought, if you were so besotted.

FIONA: I hate men, but I really hate women.

JULIA: Don't. We have to stick together. I want this to be a great evening for you.

FIONA: Oh fuck, here come some rich people, I can smell it. Tell them about how buying art makes being rich all right.

(YOYO *and* BIDDY *have come in. They look around politely.*)

BIDDY: You could buy the whole show. Right now.

YOYO: No, that would seem foreign, brash.

BIDDY: I don't think so. How are you feeling?

YOYO: Better. I still have some pain. I don't understand these.

BIDDY: You don't need to. That one's good, by a woman. She's over there. Do you want to talk to her?

YOYO: What do I say?

BIDDY: Oh, platitudes.

YOYO: Biddy, are you sure this sort of stuff would impress Sir Philip?

BIDDY: This is so exciting. She paints Greek myths.

YOYO: But darling, you know I loathe Greek myths, they're so violent. And she looks violent, male, is she, euh, a lesbian?

BIDDY: Yoyo, these are artists, it doesn't matter.

(*They go to* FIONA.)

FIONA: Hello, I'm the artist.

YOYO: How do you do. A pleasure to meet you.

BIDDY: My husband's very interested in your Greek myths.

FIONA: These two are from a series called *Solitude*. Most Greek myths are about solitude, I think.

YOYO: Oh? Yes.

(*A pause.*)

Yes.

(JULIA *joins them.*)

JULIA: Have a look at the sunsets, Mr Andreas, you will like those. Sunsets over the Thames.

YOYO: That interests me very much. I have a project on the Thames. It's a beautiful river, isn't it? I don't understand why people still resist living there.

(JEAN, *an androgynous person dressed in black, walks in, looks around critically, goes to* JEREMY.)

JEAN: What's going on?

JEREMY: Hello, Jean.

JEAN: What's the theme?

JEREMY: Mmm.

JEAN: You've got some international art, you've even got a couple of Baselitz. One Beuys drawing. And then you've got some romantic English new stuff, whatever you call it, and what's this?

JEREMY: That's also landscape. English.

JEAN: What's this with the English, Jeremy? Since when are their parochial doodles important?

JEREMY: It's the newest of the new.

JEAN: Says who? Morris? Who did you get to write your catalogue? Yeah, I thought so.

(STEPHEN *comes in.*)

JEREMY: My god, there's Stephen, I can't believe it.

JEAN: Who's he? Ah – Stephen Ryle. Why is he here? Is he important? Didn't Charles de-accession him some time ago? What's he doing?

JEREMY: Landscapes.

JEAN: The English are hopeless. Landscape. That went out fifty years ago. Fiona's sunsets, really. The Greek stuff is better, sort of a cross between Rauschenberg and Clemente. Of course Clemente's gone off too. There's only Baselitz really, yeah, Baselitz. That's the best.

JEREMY: Why?

JEAN: Because we say so, all of us. What am I going to write about this? I like you, Jeremy, you used to have good stuff.

JULIA: Call it *At the Crossroads*. Or *Buy British*.

JEAN: Yes, that's good. It's shoddy, it's parochial, it's old-fashioned, but it's British.

YOYO: You should not put down British products, they are very good, often. And we need to make them better, not give up. English history is magnificent and landscape is part of history. So many English things are admirable.

JEAN: Not the art. You're a collector, I can tell by your suit. You're in the wrong place. You could buy that Baselitz over there, it's art. Otherwise – nothing. Take my word for it, don't buy the sunsets.

STEPHEN: What do you know about art?

JULIA: Jean writes for *Elan*.

STEPHEN: What's the rag trade got to do with art?

JEAN: Everybody reads my magazine. I determine style. I tell people what's important.

STEPHEN: Why don't you just tell them to look?

JEAN: It's not enough to look with modern art. You have to understand. Good modern art must be difficult. And so it needs us – the interpreters. Art criticism is undervalued in this country, the English are so amateur about everything. In America you'll soon be able to get a degree in it.

STEPHEN: What exactly do you explain: how to match the recipes to the paintings?

JEAN: The fact is the critic these days is the equal of the artist and without the critic to point out significance and deconstruct it, the artist's work is incomplete. Every artist needs a good critic and if you don't have one, you're nothing.

STEPHEN: I'm going to vomit. You wear black and the most hideous shade of lipstick I've ever seen and you're going to discourse on the significance of colour in contemporary art?

JEAN: I've written on colour and sensuality, yes.

STEPHEN: You look as sensual as a tube of toothpaste.

JEAN: And I'm going to lecture to the Patrons of New Art. They want my advice for the Turner Prize. I certainly couldn't

35

nominate any of the stuff in here.

JULIA: Jean, you haven't looked carefully yet.

JEAN: I've seen what I need to: it's English.

YOYO: Why do you hate England so much?

JEAN: Doesn't everybody? The whole place is falling apart. Look at this gallery, it's lost its nerve.

JULIA: You mean we're not following International fashion blindly? We're not being American?

JEAN: There you go. When the English feel insecure they always attack the Americans.

JEREMY: I never attack the Americans, but I suppose I never feel insecure.

(CONSTANTIN *comes in*.)

CONSTANTIN: Hello, I am Romanian.

STEPHEN: (*To* JEAN) You're the only thing that's wrong with this country, you and your brain-damaged magazines and vapid television programmes.

MARIANNE: Stephen, you ruined your own career and now you're wrecking Fiona's.

JULIA: I've heard of collectors buying paintings they see in a magazine without even looking at the original. I think that is what Stephen is worried about.

JEAN: The English ambition: back to reading by candlelight.

CONSTANTIN: From Romania I have come to look at the paintings, are you having a political discussion?

JULIA: No, it's about art.

CONSTANTIN: Same thing, how interesting, in my country we have many discussions now and I have come for some art. I want some of your paintings.

JULIA: We'll give you a price list.

CONSTANTIN: You don't understand, I am Romanian.

STEPHEN: (*To* JEAN) Why don't you unglue your mascara and look at this show? It has two strands. One is original, rich, well painted, and then you see painters who have been reading the magazines, that one, fashion.

JEAN: That's the one I like. It's contemporary.

STEPHEN: It's badly painted.

JEAN: It's difficult. There's something to write about.

36

STEPHEN: It's bad. It's ugly. But you can write about it. Why don't you write about pots and pans and stop smearing art with your lipstick mind?

JEAN: Domestic utensils have great significance in contemporary consciousness.

STEPHEN: That's my point, everything looks the same to you. Come on, Fiona, this is a gallery for the blind.

JEAN: Beauty, you know, that's a rather old-fashioned concept. I suppose you could say Fiona's here are beautiful. So what. And those in the corner, back there. They're by you, I think.

STEPHEN: Wait a minute. Jeremy, who told you you could show my paintings here?

JEREMY: It's only three. I own them.

MARIANNE: I sold him the landscapes.

STEPHEN: Take them off the wall. Now.

CONSTANTIN: May I look at these? I am Romanian.

STEPHEN: Yes, you can have them.

JEREMY: Stephen, you can't –

STEPHEN: No, Jeremy, you can't. I don't show in this gallery any more. You dropped me.

JEREMY: I never dropped you –

STEPHEN: You dropped me from that group show.

JEREMY: You weren't in the mainstream. You wanted to do your own thing, as they said in those days. You could paint – it's just what you were painting –

STEPHEN: Didn't fit in with the dictates of *Art Forum*.

JEREMY: Stephen, watercolours . . . really, that was perverse. It was the beginning of the eighties, Thatcher, no one wanted to look at watercolours. I couldn't help that, but now, well . . .

STEPHEN: Now I wouldn't show here if you got down on your knees and licked my paintbrushes.

JEREMY: I paid your mortage.

CONSTANTIN: I like these paintings very much, yes.

JEREMY: They're very expensive.

CONSTANTIN: Good. I tell them that in Bucharest.

BIDDY: Actually, I – we – wanted to buy those paintings.

JEREMY: Ah.

STEPHEN: Who are you?

37

BIDDY: A collector. That is, my husband is.

STEPHEN: You look like the type who should be taking lessons in flower arranging.

BIDDY: (*Charmingly*) Yes, I'm very good at that.

STEPHEN: And your husband is buying you an art collection to show off instead of diamonds?

YOYO: Please, this is not polite.

BIDDY: (*To* YOYO) It's all right. (*To* STEPHEN) Well . . . in a way . . . is that wrong?

STEPHEN: Do you know what I hate about the rich? They can't spot a compliment from an insult. You buy your way out of criticism of your behaviour and you feel you can ignore the difference between good and evil – if you even remember there is a difference.

BIDDY: I was so looking forward to this evening. I thought this world would be different, not like my husband's world, the business world, where you expect to be jostled and everything to shift. I thought art would have value, I mean real value. Something eternal, reassuring, like church when I was little, or school. I know I was only invited here because I'm very rich, but I felt honoured, like paying your way into heaven if you're a Catholic. Well, why shouldn't you?

STEPHEN: Art, yes, but this world is more putrid than any hell. Your husband would be in prison if he imitated the practices of the art world. Look at Jeremy. He's going to try to convince you that the inferior work of a young painter is worth thirty thousand. And he has stuff he tries to sell for half a million you wouldn't want to pee on. You can always tell when Jeremy is putting up the price of something. He begins to put quotes before the name, a little pause, a little intake of breath. You don't just say Schnabel. You say breathe, pause, look mysterious, Schnabel. And when he does that to someone new, they've been Schnabelized. Fiona now stands in danger of being Schnabelized. But in a few years she could be dumped. A minor painter could be fashionable and envious, the two often go together. He will refuse to show with Fiona. At a foreign show, let's say. And then Fiona will begin to have a smell. A wound, and –

38

BIDDY: And that's what happened to you? The only thing is, he's beginning to put that silence around your name. And I understand why. They're beautiful.

(CONSTANTIN *comes up to* JEREMY.)

CONSTANTIN: I like these and those two over there.

JEREMY: You don't understand, it costs a lot of money.

CONSTANTIN: No, you don't understand. I am Romanian, you give me the painting. People want to give us food, blankets, but I come here to collect paintings and then I have a gallery. We are very ignorant.

STEPHEN: Here, take them. A gift to the people of Romania. Fiona will give you hers as well. Help Romania, Fiona.

MARIANNE: Stephen, you can't.

FIONA: I don't want my work to be given to the people of Romania thank you very much, and don't be such a fucking male bully.

STEPHEN: Show some guts, Fiona.

FIONA: I am showing guts, I'm painting and I'm admitting I want to be successful.

STEPHEN: You mean you're selling out?

FIONA: No, I'm buying in.

JEAN: I like that, you have a personality, I'll write about you.

JULIA: Fiona's work is very original. It takes a while to understand it. Have a careful look, Jean.

JEAN: Yes, I can see something in there, yes –

FIONA: I've gone back to myth because the modern world is so fragmented.

JEAN: I see, a distillation of modern sensibility.

CONSTANTIN: (*To* FIONA) You are an artist? We like artists. You come visit us in Romania. You are very welcome. When do I pick up the paintings?

Now I will go and look at other galleries. We Romanians, our souls are very sick, bad-nourished, you know, retarded. I think maybe this help, some painting, this remind our souls of what we have not known. Our own artists, it is as if their hands have been frozen. Maybe now they see and remember too.

London is beautiful, capitalism is beautiful. You people

39

here, so elegant, so good, you discuss things, I don't understand well, it's too quick, all about art. Beautiful. I hope that fast we learn to be like you.

STEPHEN: (*To* CONSTANTIN) Come to my studio, there's more.

JEREMY: I'm calling my lawyers.

MARIANNE: I can't stand this. Stephen, why do you always have to make scenes, ruin everything? Why is nothing sacred to you?

STEPHEN: This filthy art-world scene is not sacred to me, Marianne. Why is it to you?

MARIANNE: Because I grew up believing in it, I studied it, I loved it, because I believed in your work, because if even art is a joke, what's serious?

STEPHEN: I haven't turned art into a joke, Jeremy has. His interest in art is as convincing as Ceauşescu defending the Save the Children Fund.

CONSTANTIN: Romania is serious. Romania needs everything. I invite you all to Romania.

STEPHEN: Here's another painting, it's also quite good. It's called *Philoctetes Returns to Troy*. See that, that's me. They'll like it in Romania. I'm the model so I can give it to you. Now come and look at these.

(*He drags* CONSTANTIN *around the room.*)

No, you don't want any of these. These are awful and they'll sell for a lot of money.

CONSTANTIN: I take these too, to show them.

YOYO: Biddy, I think it's time to leave.

BIDDY: Why, Yoyo?

YOYO: This isn't distinguished. And that painter insulted you.

BIDDY: No, you don't understand. He was just being English, defensive. We'll have a great collection. I can feel it.

JULIA: Stephen, I'm coming to see you.

JEREMY: (*To the audience*) I wonder if the Medicis had to put up with these antics. I like my painters. I only want to help them. Most of them are whores. Occasionally you get an angry virgin. I think I prefer the whores. We all have to live. Great art . . . great art happens two or three times a century. But there's a fair amount of beauty around. Why should beauty be cheap? I know, people come and buy paintings because they want status, but they get beauty thrown in. That's a good deal, at any price.

Act Two

BIDDY: I remember the end of 1989 when the walls came
tumbling down. Yoyo was excited because it meant new
markets and he needed them. People walked the streets with
smiles on their faces, but there were chill winds blowing
already. I know when it happened for me. I was watching the
Channel Four news, waiting for *Brookside*, which I like
because it's so exotic, and I was about to pour myself a drink
during the *Comment*, but suddenly I heard this man talk
about Nostradamus and I listened. I listened because one of
the girls at Benenden had gone a little mad over
Nostradamus during the last year. She was a little strange
anyway, I mean her parents were odd, journalists, or
Canadians or something, but she began to talk about the
horrors of the future and she became depressed about this
thing, the future. Eventually the headmistress confiscated
her Nostradamus and told her to worry about herself not
history, that was for others, men maybe. The future, the
general future was not a problem for Benenden girls. So
when I saw this man talking about Nostradamus I listened
and he said terrible things were predicted for the nineties and
a chill came through me because everything was going so
well and we were so rich, Yoyo and me. And now Eastern
Europe was going to get rich as well so we wouldn't even
have to feel guilty or feel nervous about communism and I
was angry at this man for saying things would go badly, but
maybe I had already noticed that actually things weren't
going so well for Yoyo and he was looking worried and ill and
muttering about confidence and that was partly why I had to
do something showy like become a collector of modern art. It
was just a chill that night, a draught coming under a door,
but now I think about it a lot.

SCENE THIRTEEN: THE HERMITAGE

BIDDY, STEPHEN. STEPHEN *cleaning brushes*.

BIDDY: I hope you don't mind . . .
    (STEPHEN *doesn't answer*.)
    You don't answer the phone . . . Julia gave me the address.
    They all know you in the village. It's beautiful here. I
    thought . . . I thought it would be wilder. Inside, I mean,
    outside it is. I could hear the sea. Here it's very neat. Cosy.
    When do you stop working?
STEPHEN: I don't.
BIDDY: Don't you need the right light?
STEPHEN: I can work by electric light. I know what colours look
    like.
BIDDY: Ah – I see. You do remember me?
    Are you surprised I came?
STEPHEN: Not really . . .
    (*A silence*.)
BIDDY: Do you mind?
    (STEPHEN *doesn't answer*.)
    I suppose you think I'm a silly society lady who doesn't
    understand anything about art and I've come to amuse
    myself.
    (*Pause*.)
    Perhaps you're right, my husband is very ill at the moment
    . . . I am trying to understand art, I've been rather bitten I
    think, it's odd, and I do like your work. It makes me feel at
    home, at peace . . .
STEPHEN: It's not for sale.
BIDDY: Are you really giving it all to Romania?
STEPHEN: If Jeremy's sent you you can go straight back –
BIDDY: No . . . I swear. Why are you so angry?
STEPHEN: Why aren't you?
BIDDY: I have nothing to be angry about. I'm married. I'm rich. I
    have a lovely big garden. I know, you're thinking what about
    others, the ones who've been betrayed, the ones who suffer
    . . . the Albanians . . . I can't be angry about that. I'm sorry,

about the famines in Africa, the homeless, all that, but it's not my fault. It's nobody fault, is it?

Is it?

Now I've made you even angrier. I mean now that we know that communism doesn't work, we know there have to be famines, don't we? Do you believe in God?

STEPHEN: You don't mean that question.

BIDDY: I wish I did, because then the famines would be God's will and that's all right. Now it just seems the luck of the draw. You see, I do think about these things. Good and evil. Although I admit I don't think about them well. I wasn't trained to.

STEPHEN: Nobody knows how to think about them any more . . .

BIDDY: I actually want to be good. Women's magazines, they tell you how to be thin, charming, cook well, even how to have a brilliant career, but not how to be good.

(*A pause.*)

Nobody talks about being good. I think once or twice I've seen the question raised in a political article Yoyo reads. But I can't see the connection. Yoyo supports the Tories, but he doesn't think they're good.

STEPHEN: Maybe he's supporting the wrong party.

BIDDY: The Labour Party is so snobbish, they wouldn't want his money. The good. I don't even know what the word means. I'm sorry, I'm talking about myself. It's funny about artists, you want to confess to them. It's because I saw something in those paintings at Jeremy's that I was looking for all the time. I can't explain. Do you? Think about the word 'good'?

STEPHEN: Look at a Titian. A Poussin. A Turner. Maybe it's not the good, but it's wonder, and that's a start.

BIDDY: Isn't there anybody modern? Besides you.

STEPHEN: You'll have to find that for yourself. And then you can buy cheap and sell at great prices. Moral questions have been out of fashion for ten years, maybe they'll come back into vogue. For six months.

BIDDY: Why do you despise everybody? How can you paint if you're so full of hate?

STEPHEN: I'm not full of hate, I'm disappointed. Twenty years ago I knew exactly what was right for the world: what art, what politics. I'm not sure about anything any more. I sometimes worry that painting trees is a sign of exhaustion rather than renewal. As for my politics . . . a rubbed-out canvas in a corner somewhere.

BIDDY: Your landscapes, they're not exactly landscapes . . .

STEPHEN: It's my contribution to history. I paint what is vanishing. As it vanishes. Sometimes I only paint the memory of something that was there long ago. A shape. We drool over the Aborigines because they hold their land sacred. But we must have all done that once. Even the English. Particularly the English. Islands are mysterious, our land is so watery, that is its beauty. You don't understand a word I'm saying.

BIDDY: Not yet, but I will, Stephen . . . I promise . . .

(*A silence. They look at each other.*)

Sometimes I feel I have two pairs of eyelids. The first pair are like everyone else's, but behind them, there's clingfilm, and if I could open those too, I would see the world differently. Maybe the way you do.

STEPHEN: You wouldn't want that.

BIDDY: I would like this blur removed. It's not really a blur, it's a flatness. Nothing is more in focus than anything else. You're an artist. That's what you do, isn't it? Perspective?

STEPHEN: I'm a modern artist, my world is as fragmented as yours. I'm in pieces.

BIDDY: You never paint figures? People?

STEPHEN: Is that what you want? Is that what you came for?

BIDDY: Oh, no, please, I wouldn't dream . . . dare, no, I'm not vain. Yoyo always says he wants to have our portraits done, I think he imagines a kind of Gainsborough, lots of green land, me in a hat, but no. . .

(STEPHEN *goes towards her.*)

STEPHEN: I wouldn't paint your portrait. I would find your Significant Form.

BIDDY: What's that?

STEPHEN: I don't know yet.

45

SCENE FOURTEEN: VALUE ADDED

MR BOREMAN, MRS BOREMAN, JEREMY, NICOLA.

MR BOREMAN: The first Mrs Boreman and I met him at your
private view. I think he was on drugs. He mumbled a lot and
he was very rude to my then-wife. Still, I was very sorry to
hear of his death. His stuff was rocketing through the roof,
but I thought, no, I'll wait.
(*A pause.*)

JEREMY: Mm, waiting, yes . . .

MR BOREMAN: But I don't like it. Fact is I never did. Too much,
too much . . . yellow. It was my ex-wife, I don't think she
looked at it much, she liked the idea of it, because he was
black, from the slums, she was one of those guilty liberals.

JEREMY: Mmm.

MR BOREMAN: Anyhow, you convinced us.

JEREMY: I . . .?

MR BOREMAN: I remember your very words. Savage. Noble. The
genetic imprint of the jungle.

JEREMY: I said that?

MR BOREMAN: I should have known then. I took a trip to the
jungle when I was in Brazil. I hated it. Too, too . . . green.

JEREMY: Mmm. Green.

MR BOREMAN: Anyway, the new Mrs Boreman doesn't like it, do
you, dear?

MRS BOREMAN: I hate it.

JEREMY: Ah, yes, I see, that happens: redecoration. You can
always put it in another room.

MR BOREMAN: My wife says it reminds her of graffiti.

JEREMY: I think that's what it is supposed to do. The genius of
the people.

MR BOREMAN: Yes, but Mrs Boreman is from the people herself.

MRS BOREMAN: I'm from the working class.

JEREMY: I thought you were American.

MRS BOREMAN: I am American and I'm from the working class.
My father worked in a factory. I grew up on the wrong side
of the tracks in a small town that had a college. I was bright,

so I got a scholarship. I don't need graffiti on my walls. I like Constable. Gainsborough.

JEREMY: Not many of those about.

MR BOREMAN: Well, do you have anything like that? But contemporary.

JEREMY: I might.

MR BOREMAN: I'd like to make an exchange.

JEREMY: An exchange? Ah. I'm afraid that's not possible.

MR BOREMAN: I paid two hundred and fifty thousand dollars for it, it must be worth much more than that now. Have you got something for three hundred thousand, four hundred thousand?

JEREMY: Yes. But we don't exchange . . . We aren't Marks and Spencers.

MRS BOREMAN: Why don't you just take it back and give us the money.

MR BOREMAN: Dear, let me . . . but that's an idea.

JEREMY: Buy it back? I'm – well, cash flow, as you people say . . . These artists, I'm supporting so many of them, they're so lazy . . .

MR BOREMAN: Sell it for me, then.

JEREMY: I don't know what I could get . . . People are cautious these days.

MR BOREMAN: This stuff is supposed to go up and up. That's what you told me.

JEREMY: No. I'd never say anything so practical.

MR BOREMAN: I heard that said here. That's why I bought it.

JEREMY: That must have been my assistant. Michael. I had to get rid of him. Some of my assistants had the souls of city people. Now Nicola would never say anything like that.
(NICOLA *shakes her head*.)

MRS BOREMAN: What exactly would you have said, Nicola?

JEREMY: She would have said you must only buy a painting because you love it, wouldn't you, Nicola?
(NICOLA *nods*.)

MRS BOREMAN: It's hard to know what you love when all these people are telling you what you're supposed to love. I used to love that girl in the cornfield by Andrew Wyeth, you know,

47

Christina's House, the print of it. Then I heard I was
supposed to love the Abstract Expressionists. I got to love
Rothko and after ten years of trying I even love Jasper Johns.

MR BOREMAN: I've looked into Jasper Johns. Eight million.

JEREMY: And there's a queue.

MRS BOREMAN: But this guy, even if he cost forty million I
wouldn't love him. I hate this painting.

JEREMY: Odd about this painter. He had everything going for him:
young, black, new, there wasn't much else that year, he even
died young, very good of him, in a business sense, but . . .

MR BOREMAN: But?

JEREMY: It's so difficult . . . His paintings should be selling for
three-quarters of a million by now. But they're not. Why?
Sometimes you make a mistake. The value of the stock goes
down. I suppose it's loss of confidence. We may have sold his
paintings to the wrong people. I mean, he's not in the most
famous collections. Some of the people who bought his
paintings are now in prison. All those stock-market scandals.
It's not good. People change. And then some critics laid into
him. Mmm. We're all a slave to fashion.

MRS BOREMAN: I thought we were talking about painting.

MR BOREMAN: We're also talking two hundred and fifty thousand
dollars here. Are you saying you sold me shoddy goods?

JEREMY: No, the canvas hasn't disintegrated. It isn't like
Schnabel's plates all falling off. And his stuff is still worth
millions, even without the plates.

MRS BOREMAN: We're not asking for plates. We want some art.

JEREMY: There's my dosser. I've told him always to make
sure no one's here. I'm usually closed at this time.
(*He rushes out.*)
Vincent, I told you . . .
(*A silence.* NICOLA *looks up, smiles.*)

NICOLA: Art is very mysterious.

MRR BOREMAN: Nicola, when Mr Bertrand sold my husband
that painting what was it really worth?

NICOLA: It was worth what you paid for it.

MRS BOREMAN: You mean because that's what we were prepared
to pay for it?

48

NICOLA: No – well, yes.

MR BOREMAN: And what is it worth now?

NICOLA: What somebody else might be prepared to pay for it.

MR BOREMAN: And what's that?

NICOLA: That could be nothing.

(JEREMY *comes back.*)

JEREMY: The Strand's full, so the homeless are moving up Cork
Street. I have a deal with him: I don't let anyone else occupy
the doorway, but he leaves as soon as the gallery opens in the
morning and doesn't come until I've left. Vincent – he's
rather nice. Young. I wouldn't want one of those fat bag
ladies. He seems to like the art. Twenty years ago he might
have got a grant and gone to art school or a polytechnic. I
think we valued potential more in those days. It's like your
poor artist here. He wasn't much of a painter, but he might
have become one, or a media star, like Warhol, it's just as
good, so we all valued his potential. But potential itself lost
value. What can I do? I'm just an ordinary art dealer. I'm
terribly sorry, Mr and Mrs Boreman, but Vincent needs his
doorway.

(*He pushes them out gently, with the painting.*)

SCENE FIFTEEN: THE PRICE OF EVERYTHING

A doctor's office. White walls, an antique bust. MR MERCER *and*
BIDDY.

BIDDY: I thought I'd come first. And then I can convince him that
it will be simple and comfortable.

(MR MERCER *nods.*)

He couldn't stand a machine, you know. He doesn't like –
well, the insides of a body, the mess. He's very clean, very
private. Very discreet.

(MR MERCER *nods.*)

But if he can just go to sleep and wake up completely well.

(*A silence. The doctor looks through some notes, as doctors do.*)

MR MERCER: I have one coming in that would match.

BIDDY: Oh, that's wonderful.

49

MR MERCER: Of course, I would have to see your husband.

BIDDY: Oh, yes. Is it terribly expensive? You see if I paid for it myself, it would – well, the decision would have been made. I have quite a lot of money at my disposal, I was going to buy a painting, but I can do that later.

MR MERCER: You like art? So do I. I collect antique statuary. And you?

BIDDY: I'm just starting.

MR MERCER: I have a very good contact if you go for the Med.

BIDDY: The Med?

MR MERCER: (*Points to his bust*) That sort of thing. Cradle of civilization.

BIDDY: Oh, yes, yes . . .

(*A silence.*)

MR MERCER: The kidney itself costs two thousand five hundred pounds.

BIDDY: Is that all? I mean – well. But, will it be a good – I mean, at that price . . . I'd be willing to pay more, if there's a better one going, you know.

(*A pause.*)

It is English?

MR MERCER: I'm afraid not, Mrs Andreas. You can only get an English kidney when somebody dies in an accident and then it goes straight to the National Health. The relatives are usually happy to give the organs away. There's a long queue for kidneys and the National Health favours young people, whereas I suppose you could say private medicine favours useful members of society like your husband.

BIDDY: So these – euh – come from . . .

MR MERCER: Somebody who is quite happy to give a kidney away, at a price of course. It may not be such a good idea to have someone who lives in this country, in case they change their minds. That would be awkward. Having to give it back.

(*He laughs. A silence.*)

BIDDY: Where does the – euh – it come from?

MR MERCER: We get them from Turkey. But I assure you they come from very healthy specimens. I have a long list, Mrs

50

Andreas, if you would prefer to wait . . . but I can't
guarantee anything, I just happen to have this one coming in.
Today.

BIDDY: Do you have it here? I mean, euh . . .

MR MERCER: I have the man over here. He can be operated on in a
few days and we will give it straightaway to your husband, who
should then be able to lead a healthy life for years to come.

BIDDY: This man, he's all right, is he? I mean, he's not a criminal?
I'm sorry, I know so little about medicine, I suppose it doesn't
matter, it's not the brain, is it? It's just that – Well, yes, fine. I
couldn't – euh – meet him? I'd feel better.
(*A pause.*)
I'm afraid otherwise I couldn't, I simply wouldn't be sure . . .

MR MERCER: It's unusual, but I suppose you can, he's in my
waiting room. The operation itself is only one thousand, but
seven days in hospital, fifteen hundred pounds a night for a
private room, that will be – (*he takes out a calculator*) –
fourteen thousand. You only need deposit half of that. Non-
returnable if you change your mind as we have to save the
room.

BIDDY: I understand. Of course. (*She takes out her cheque book.*)
Who do I make it out to? I mean, do I make out two cheques,
one for the – euh – ?

MR MERCER: No, we take care of all that.

BIDDY: It isn't very much for a kidney, is it?

MR MERCER: It's the going rate. There are lots of them about.
(MR MERCER *goes to call* AHMET. BIDDY *looks at the ancient
bust.* MR MERCER *comes back in, sees this.*)
That comes from Turkey too. But it's unique. And very
expensive. There are two more by the same sculptor and my
obsession is to find them. Get them. I dream about it at night.
Touch it, Mrs Andreas.
(BIDDY *touches it.*)
You have touched the antique world, the mid-morning of
civilization. A sculptor moulded these features more than two
thousand years ago, a sculptor who spoke to Plato, who fought
Sparta, who knew Alcibiades.

BIDDY: I see, yes. It's very smooth. Doctor, I must ask you one thing.

MR MERCER: I don't know who the model was, a young soldier I
  think. Here's Ahmet.
  (AHMET, *a young Turk, comes in. He is clearly baffled and does
  not understand much or any English.*)
  Ahmet, this is Mrs Andreas. Your kidney is going to be
  given to her husband.
  (AHMET *nods, smiles, bows.*)
  You understand? Your kidney.
  (AHMET *smiles.*)
BIDDY: It's – euh – very kind of you, I mean, well, we're very
  grateful.
AHMET: No problem. No problem.
MR MERCER: And Mrs Andreas is giving you the money for your
  mother. The money.
BIDDY: Yes, I hope it's – euh, well – I'm very pleased to meet you.
  (*She stretches out her hand.* AHMET *seizes it and kisses it.*)
  I hope you don't mind the operation. My husband is
  frightened.
  (*She mimics fear by miming cold.*)
AHMET: No problem for Ahmet. Yes. No problem.
  (*They all smile.*)
MR MERCER: Good boy.
  (AHMET *laughs.*)
AHMET: Yes. Yes.
BIDDY: He's very sweet. (*To* AHMET) I hear Turkey is very
  beautiful. Beautiful.
  (*She points to her eyes.* AHMET *looks in panic at* MR MERCER,
  shakes his head and covers his eyes with his hands.)
MR MERCER: No, Ahmet, only one kidney.
  (*He points to his side, ushers him out.*)
  He thought you wanted his eyes as well.
BIDDY: He does understand what he's doing?
MR MERCER: Oh, yes, he's signed the form.
BIDDY: Mr Mercer, when you speak to my husband, please don't
  tell him the – the – euh – the kidney – is Turkish. You see,
  he is Greek, and you know, the history of the Ottoman
  domination, well, he takes it personally. He might reject a
  Turkish organ.

The gardens of Kenwood House on Hampstead Heath. JULIA *and* MARIANNE *are sitting, waiting.* BIDDY *joins them.*

MARIANNE: Sometimes I think I'm going to find it. I've done counselling, yoga, I've seen a medium, I've had my chart read, I do visualization every morning. Nothing. I can't have children any more, I have twenty, maybe thirty years left. What am I going to do? I get vertigo at the thought. I see Lady Lelouche and the Romanian. Why are we here, Julia?

JULIA: One of Lady Lelouche's causes. It can't be too important because she's invited us to a concert at Kenwood instead of Glyndebourne.

MARIANNE: It can't be too important because she's invited us full stop.

BIDDY: This is much more fun than Glyndebourne. There are children here. I seem to be on so many lists. I go to everything because I keep thinking the art world will make me more intelligent. Sometimes I feel I'm still at a hunt ball, the talk. I expected something more moral.

JULIA: Morality? In the art world? You sound like Stephen.
    (LADY LELOUCHE *approaches with* CONSTANTIN.)

CONSTANTIN: What a beautiful house there, very beautiful.

LADY LELOUCHE: All my dissidents love Kenwood, it's so graceful.

CONSTANTIN: You own it, Lady Lelouche?

LADY LELOUCHE: I only help administer it. It belongs to the public. The concert will begin in twenty minutes, we can chat until then.

CONSTANTIN: A concert yes, I love outdoor concerts. The Sex Pistols, the Beatles too.

BIDDY: Sibelius Violin Concerto.

LADY LELOUCHE: There's a piece by Bartók. Same general area as you, I thought you might enjoy it.

MARIANNE: Were you in prison for long?

CONSTANTIN: Yes, all of Romania is a prison.

MARIANNE: Were you tortured?

CONSTANTIN: I suffer very much. My poor country . . .

LADY LELOUCHE: That's what Constantin wants to talk to us about. He is very concerned about the monasteries in his country.

JULIA: We could organize an exhibition of icons. Jeremy might do it in his gallery or I could find a space myself with your help, Lady Lelouche.

CONSTANTIN: I find you some icons but these monasteries are beautiful because they are painted. On the outside. They are small, all covered outside like embroidered vestments.

LADY LELOUCHE: My mother used to dance the carnival in Bucharest, but she went to the monasteries. She loved them. Very handsome monks.

CONSTANTIN: Ceauşescu wanted to destroy them.

LADY LELOUCHE: We did something about that, slapped a UNESCO order or something.

CONSTANTIN: Now they are in bad neglect, and the vandalism and also very bad pollution.

LADY LELOUCHE: You people must do something about your pollution. It's ruining the rest of Europe, not to mention the Danube.

CONSTANTIN: We need much help and money. There are five monasteries and they are famous for colour. The most famous, Voronetz, has blue, a blue that goes dark in the rain. The colour is a secret, they do not know how to ever get it back. This church, painted in the sixteenth century, has – we call it the Sistine Chapel of the East – it has a Last Judgement. Another, Humor, has all the episodes of the Akathistos, you know the Akathistos? An Orthodox long prayer before Holy Week. So the painting is also a story: every square like a chapter.

BIDDY: Yoyo's mother sent him an icon once, I don't know where he's hidden it.

MARIANNE: I like the sound of it. Narrative art.

CONSTANTIN: The churches have red, green, each different. The monasteries are small villages. You eat well there, and artists go and rest.

MARIANNE: Who painted all this?

54

CONSTANTIN: That is the beauty, no name, they were monks. They were protected by Stephen the Great, you know Stephen the Great, our hero? Every time he won a battle against the Turks, he built another church.

BIDDY: Yoyo will like that.

LADY LELOUCHE: You have something interesting there, Constantin. The next step would be for you to give a lecture.

MARIANNE: I could help you write it, I'm good at that. Julia, we can use the gallery mailing list. I love the idea of anonymous art.

LADY LELOUCHE: Mrs Andreas?

BIDDY: I'm happy to give a little money. We're slightly overstretched . . .

LADY LELOUCHE: I hear you've been buying some very new paintings.

BIDDY: I can't buy what I really want.

MARIANNE: He still won't sell?

(BIDDY *shakes her head.*)

JULIA: It's because of Jeremy. Without Jeremy we'd be all right.

LADY LELOUCHE: The concert is about to begin. Constantin, when I spoke to you in Romania you said you were getting slides. The light is still good enough and I've brought my glass.

CONSTANTIN: Slides, yes, I show you.

(*He takes out two crumpled papers and shows them.*)

LADY LELOUCHE: No, *slides.*

CONSTANTIN: Yes, slides: here, beautiful. Here is Voronetz.

LADY LELOUCHE: But this is just some pages torn from a book. Rather greasy I might say and coffee-stained.

MARIANNE: Slides are colour photographs, which you look through.

CONSTANTIN: These are very good, taken twenty years ago by French man. Very good book. The only book on our monasteries.

LADY LELOUCHE: I can't raise money for monasteries with two pieces of paper.

CONSTANTIN: But I talk too. I give good lecture. Marianne help me.

LADY LELOUCHE: People supported the orphans because they saw them on television, it wouldn't have done any good just describing them. There's a lot of competition for people's sympathy.

MARIANNE: Why not alert the television news, Lady Lelouche?

LADY LELOUCHE: You might get monasteries on the news if they were being demolished, but that would defeat the purpose, wouldn't it?

CONSTANTIN: Well, they come to Romania and I show them.

LADY LELOUCHE: My dear man, Romania is very uncomfortable and there's nothing to eat. I simply couldn't invite The Friends of the Tate to see some torn-out pages of a book. Come back when you have slides. I'm sorry to have wasted your time, Mrs Andreas. I thought that because of your husband and his architecture . . .

BIDDY: Please . . .

LADY LELOUCHE: But we have a marvellous lecture next Monday. Constantin, you will have to understand that in the West we expect people to be – how shall I say – professional. I've always been very impressed by the professionalism of dissidents.

CONSTANTIN: I am Romanian.

LADY LELOUCHE: Yes, but what exactly does that mean?

CONSTANTIN: You do not know what it is to lose your soul for twenty-five years. We had Ceauşescu, yes, but we were all little Ceauşescus. Now we do not know how to begin, we look around, we know nothing and we are ashamed. I know what a slide is. How can I have slides when I do not have a camera, or film, when we have no scaffolding to get close to the painting and it is crumbling every day?

MARIANNE: This is terrible. We have to help.

LADY LELOUCHE: I'm beginning to sense Romania is one of those hopeless causes.

MARIANNE: I'm very good at hopeless causes. I was married to one. And I take very good pictures. Yes, I'm going to Romania to save the monasteries. Constantin, we'll do it on our own if we have to.

JULIA: I'll come and look at the contemporary art.

CONSTANTIN: Biddy, you come too?
BIDDY: I love England at the moment . . .

SCENE SEVENTEEN: PHILOCTETES, PART TWO

NEOPTOLEMUS *and, hidden,* ODYSSEUS *in disguise.*

NEOPTOLEMUS: Bleak. I'm glad I don't live here. What do I
    hear? It's a moan.
    (PHILOCTETES/STEPHEN *enters, limping.*)
PHILOCTETES: A human being. A Greek. Who are you? What are
    you doing here. Not many people come here.
NEOPTOLEMUS: Neoptolemus. Son of Achilles. Victim of
    Odysseus.
ODYSSEUS: (*Aside*) I love the young. They're so eager, so
    corruptible.
PHILOCTETES: Your father was a friend. How is he?
NEOPTOLEMUS: Dead.
PHILOCTETES: He didn't want to go to the war, he knew he'd die
    young. I wanted to go. How's Ajax?
NEOPTOLEMUS: Dead.
PHILOCTETES: Mm. The wise Nestor?
NEOPTOLEMUS: His son's died.
PHILOCTETES: And your father's friend Patroclus?
NEOPTOLEMUS: Dead.
PHILOCTETES: Naturally the evil Agamemnon and the cuckold
    Menelaus who started the war are alive?
    (NEOPTOLEMUS *nods.*)
    And the liar Odysseus?
NEOPTOLEMUS: Alive. He took my father's arms, you know that
    famous shield everyone talks about. So I left. He tried to stop
    me. I need my father's arms, I can't fight without them, it's
    all I have. But you must excuse me, I don't know who you
    are.
PHILOCTETES: Philoctetes.
NEOPTOLEMUS: *The* Philoctetes? The Philoctetes with the
    famous bow and arrows? Can I look?
    (*He admires the bow and arrows.*)

57

Can I touch? Could I just try one . . .

PHILOCTETES: I'm not as great a fighter as your father, but with these, I'm invincible.

NEOPTOLEMUS: I hate Odysseus. I could kill him with these.

ODYSSEUS: He's overdoing it.

(*He rushes on, covering his face.*)

ODYSSEUS/SEAMAN: Neoptolemus, I've seen a ship and I'm sure it's Odysseus pursuing you. Get back to your ship quickly. Run.

PHILOCTETES: Let me come with you. Off this cursed island.

ODYSSEUS/SEAMAN: Who are you, beggar?

NEOPTOLEMUS: That's the famous Philoctetes.

ODYSSEUS/SEAMAN: Odysseus told everyone that after he'd caught Neoptolemus, he'd come and get you and drag you back to Troy.

PHILOCTETES: I'll never go back. Take me with you, Neoptolemus. Ah, this pain. The sore's opened again. It's when I get upset. It's the name of Odysseus.

ODYSSEUS: We can't have him on the ship, he stinks.

PHILOCTETES: Take me, throw me overboard, but get me off this island. Aie, aie. Wait.

ODYSSEUS: Why don't you take his bow and arrows, Neoptolemus, he'll walk more easily.

NEOPTOLEMUS: No, I can't.

PHILOCTETES: Yes, do, please. Help me.

NEOPTOLEMUS: I can't. I can't go on with this, this is vile.

ODYSSEUS: There's a war on. In times of crisis, trust your leaders.

PHILOCTETES: O gods, why have you cursed me? I was the best warrior Troy had.

NEOPTOLEMUS: I'm going to tell him the truth.

ODYSSEUS: You don't know the truth. We're tricking him, but how do you know his own soul doesn't want to return to Troy?

NEOPTOLEMUS: I don't understand.

PHILOCTETES: Odysseus, I recognize the shape of your words.

SCENE EIGHTEEN: BLACK

Sound of a shop alarm. RUSSET *ushers* YOYO *into a small room, indicates a chair.*

RUSSET: And now I shall have to ask you a few questions, if you don't mind, sir.

YOYO: I was hot . . .

(RUSSET *takes out a form.*)

No. Please. I can't answer. I was only looking at it in the light . . . no. You don't understand. I am a rich man. I have a business.

RUSSET: Are you having trouble with your business, sir?

YOYO: Yes, of course, like every one else, too much borrowing. The interest rates. Prince Charles doesn't like my buildings on the river. He disapproves of the materials. If the press – they're always after us. Please. It takes years to build up a business, but twenty-four hours can tumble it – you know.

RUSSET: Your name?

YOYO: No . . . Andreas, Mr Andreas. This mustn't – I'm a member of the Progress Club. In my closet I have three coats from Harrods, one like this one, better, you must believe me.

RUSSET: I do believe you, sir. Perhaps you can tell me what happened.

YOYO: I tried it on. It didn't even fit very well. My wife usually comes with me – she mustn't –

RUSSET: Are you having difficulties with your wife, sir?

YOYO: No, we've been married four years. She's lovely, very English, pale . . .

RUSSET: Is there another woman, perhaps, sir?

YOYO: Only in so far as is usual with men in the city. I can't talk to my wife about – hard things, architecture. This is such a bad year. And she's spending so much money, she didn't before, but we're art collectors . . . I have a lot of pain too. Kidneys. I have great faith in English medicine, but it is not as good as it was.

RUSSET: You have a kidney problem, sir?

YOYO: Just pain . . . it's worry.

RUSSET: So you've been under a lot of pressure.

YOYO: Yes . . . but please, don't write it. I relax at the club, but the conversation is not as interesting as I thought it would be. There are too many thrusters. Young businessmen, they want to talk about money. And the old ones about Europe. I want to talk about England. But the library is beautiful. I could take you to lunch there, of course without your uniform.

RUSSET: (*Coldly*) So you say you were trying on the coat. And then?

YOYO: I can't remember.

RUSSET: You put it on your arm, under your jacket. And then you walked out of the store.

YOYO: I didn't – think.

RUSSET: I believe you did think, Mr Andreas, I believe you thought you could get away with it.

YOYO: No. I'm a rich man.

RUSSET: I've worked four years in this store and I've observed this about the rich, the very rich I'm talking about, they think they can get away with it, they think they're above the law, you should see the people we get here, titles, princesses, everything, usually women, but more and more men.

YOYO: I haven't been rich all my life. I've worked hard. I don't – I'm not like that.

RUSSET: Then why are you trying to bribe me?

YOYO: Bribe you? No. You mean the Club? No, no, it's so you'll understand I am a gentleman.

(*Pause.*)

RUSSET: I think you need counselling.

YOYO: Sorry? Sometimes I have so much pain, I can't hear.

RUSSET: Harrods offers most services to its customers, but it hasn't opened a counselling service yet. I can give you the name of a doctor.

YOYO: Please, I have so many doctors, I'm going into hospital.

(*Pause.*)

I love England. Please don't write anything down.

RUSSET: Your doctor's name?

YOYO: I can't remember. Murder . . . no, Mercer.

RUSSET: I will need to take your photograph.

YOYO: No! (*He starts crying.*) I'm sorry. It's not very – stiff upper lip –

RUSSET: Listen. I'm going to let you go. I don't know why, but I am. I don't think you're a habitual shoplifter, you're what I call a crisis shoplifter. But I will have to ask you one thing.

YOYO: On my honour.

RUSSET: I shall have to ask you, sir, never, as long as you live, to set foot in Harrods again.

YOYO: But my wife – we love coming here. The food halls – the fish –

RUSSET: May I ask you, sir, to hand me the coat.
(YOYO *hands the coat he has been clutching.*)
And the silver letter-opener.

SCENE NINETEEN: PHILOCTETES RETURNS TO TROY

A large canvas in Stephen's studio. STEPHEN, JEREMY, ALEX,
GWEN. JEREMY *stares at the canvas.* ALEX *rummages around.*

JEREMY: You've been angry for a long time. Ten years ago people wanted Chia, Clemente, subjectivity. Artists who could say like Baselitz that art is asocial. When I look at it now I have to agree with you, most of it was meaningless, so the world wanted something meaningless in its art. Maybe it reflected the emptiness of its own self-absorption. What you were doing didn't speak to anybody. So we did drop you. Maybe it was wrong, but right and wrong in a subjective society have no meaning either. I don't know if they do now, but there is a change, we need to redefine ourselves and you, in some way, seem to touch something. I look at what you're doing and it fills me with longing. You must want to show your work.

ALEX: This one's great. English.

STEPHEN: Ireland. I painted that of Ireland.

ALEX: Well, you English own Ireland, don't you? Anyway, you used to. And this one, wow, boy, you could be famous, I mean famous.

STEPHEN: I was famous.

ALEX: Well, isn't it great to be famous? What's wrong with you English? People in America will die to be famous. Think about it, Stephen, a major exhibition. It'll be like Jasper Johns and the American Flag. Stephen Ryle and the English Landscape. Are you afraid or what?

GWEN: Daddy, why don't you want to be famous? We could be rich and you could buy me clothes and a car. Otherwise I'll have to wait for a husband.

ALEX: Earn these things for yourself.

GWEN: I'm not ending up a feminist!

STEPHEN: Why not?

GWEN: Because *Vogue* says they're out.

ALEX: French *Vogue* says they're back in.

GWEN: Really, can I see it? Except it'll be in French. I studied French at school so I don't know a word.

JEREMY: Stephen . . . The world needs you. The art world, I don't know about the other world, I don't know what it is . . .

JULIA: There are galleries where people don't feel intimidated – they're warm, people are friendly, the paintings are there to be looked at, not always sold to someone rich. That's the kind of gallery you need.

JEREMY: I'm going to tell the girl at my desk to be more forthcoming in future.

JULIA: Your gallery's in the wrong place. Stephen, if you stay cooped up much longer you could regress. Work gets mouldy.

ALEX: Yes, and your roof will rot. The termites will eat your foundations.

JEREMY: Alex, we don't have termites in England.

ALEX: Well, whatever the English equivalent is.

JEREMY: Damp. No, actually, its drought. Rather it's the change from damp to drought.

ALEX: What?

JEREMY: That undermines foundations. It's the extremes.

England doesn't like extremes. Well, English houses don't. It's rude . . . We wouldn't have allowed the Alps in this country. Wales is bad enough.

ALEX: Maybe you enjoy being poor. I know people who love being failures. They know where they are and they hate everything. It's easy.

(CONSTANTIN *and* BIDDY *come in.*)

BIDDY: I'm sorry . . . Constantin said you'd invited him and he doesn't have a car. I didn't know . . . shall we leave?

STEPHEN: Stay, I need your advice.

BIDDY: Mine?

(*A pause.*)

They want you back?

STEPHEN: What do you think?

BIDDY: Oh . . .

CONSTANTIN: I have come to look at your paintings to take them back to Romania, thank you.

ALEX: Wait a minute, who are you?

CONSTANTIN: I am Romanian.

ALEX: I can see that, but who are you?

JEREMY: I love the Americans. I could never have asked that question.

CONSTANTIN: I have paintings to show to our people in Bucharest.

ALEX: Where?

CONSTANTIN: I don't know yet, we arrange that.

ALEX: When?

CONSTANTIN: Soon. We get help.

ALEX: When? In ten years time when you straighten the country out?

JEREMY: What happens to Stephen's paintings in the meantime?

ALEX: Same thing as the toys which disappear? Warehouses of books which never surface? Food and blankets rotting on the black market?

JULIA: Alex is right. Can you tell us exactly what you were doing during Ceauşescu's regime?

CONSTANTIN: I was . . . making do . . .

STEPHEN: How?

CONSTANTIN: But now I am businessman, like him. And you said I could take these paintings – please.

JULIA: I don't think Stephen wants to give his paintings to a Romanian version of Jeremy.

JEREMY: Corki Street.

STEPHEN: I thought you were serious. I wanted to help. I felt for the death of your students.

CONSTANTIN: Yes, I understand. I – we disappoint you. We are not doing things right, we are not pure. The trouble for us is we have to carry your dreams, your ideals, always. You were on the left in your country, no? You believed in socialism, even communism, no? That's what I thought. You are the worse. I don't mind the silly society ladies – I never really expected to get help from them because we Romanians are not chic, I know that. But you – you never came to Romania when we were communist. You preach communism in your country, but you let us make the experiment for you. So we have the destroyed land in co-operatives, the bread tails, but it doesn't matter, because we are your ideal. And when it has completely failed, and we have a revolution, you love us because we are having a revolution and that is exciting to you, even if it is a revolution against what you are preaching for in your country. And again we carry your soul for you. And now you're unhappy because we are not perfect revolutionaries, because we have not wiped out all the Securitate people, which is most of Romanians, because we are not completely good. You forgive your own evil because you say it's built into capitalism, but we are not allowed. We have to be moral, perfect martyrs.

You come and watch us, you say we are not good to our babies. You want us to have habits like people who have been well fed, with love, with toys, things we never know about and we are just so happy we are not under Ceauşescu, that is enough for us, that we are less frightened. Now you don't want me to have your paintings because I am not great dissident hero. Where were you when they were beating and killing us? You despise me because I want to live. You socialist? I go walk in the garden now.

Biddy, you pick me up when you are ready. And you Stephen, artist, you blush, not me.

(*A silence.*)

ALEX: Latins, they love to talk. Mind you, better than the English, who don't.

(BIDDY *looks at the canvas.*)

BIDDY: You didn't show me this before.

STEPHEN: I may not have been thinking very well in the last ten years, but I have been looking. Working.

BIDDY: Explain it . . .

STEPHEN: It's not an answer, it's not a solution . . .

BIDDY: I know.

STEPHEN: At the most it's a suggestion.

BIDDY: Please . . . take us through it.

STEPHEN: Go from right to left. It is about landscape. Not a literal landscape: shapes that repeat themselves in nature. Here, a tree, a field, a cloud. The energies of nature are advancing, pressing. You should know it is English because there is so much green. Earth colours too. Move to the left and these colours, forms are countered by a strict and more conventional geometry. The colours are warmer here, it is a man-made arrangement. I've always been fascinated by architecture . . . here is stability around which our lives and emotions can circulate. It's an affirmation and, in an age of cynicism, that requires some courage.

(*A silence.*)

GWEN: Daddy, don't move.

(*She frames the picture with her hands.*)

ALEX: I'm submitting this for the Constable Prize and booking you for an interview.

JEREMY: Don't overdo it.

ALEX: I know artists. Somewhere they've always got a streak of responsibility. Stephen wouldn't be spending ten hours a day on something this big if he was gonna hide it for ever. Or he really would have to blush.

JULIA: I don't think you should go back to Jeremy. You need a new gallery.

JEREMY: What are you talking about, Julia?

JULIA: I'm starting my own gallery. Fiona's coming.

JEREMY: You! But – well – you're . . . Where will you get the backing?

JULIA: When I get the artists, I'll get the backing. Alex is going to help and my father is rich, Jeremy. I suppose you thought he was a bus conductor.

JEREMY: I never thought anything.

JULIA: Exactly.

JEREMY: Julia, you can't strike out on your own. Look, why don't we get married? You wouldn't have to, as you know I don't – we could have a partnership like the de Clares. I can't do it on my own, I don't know how to see any more. You should get married. It would make you belong more.

JULIA: I don't need you for that.

STEPHEN: (*To* BIDDY) That's the world you want me to go back to?

BIDDY: I never asked you.

STEPHEN: But you did.

BIDDY: Did I? I'm sorry. No, you're right. I did. I wanted it. And I'm not sorry.

GWEN: Daddy, now that you're going back to the real world and Mummy's going to Romania for ever to save the monasteries, you will look after me? I'm all alone.

SCENE TWENTY: BLACK ON BLACK

An elegant private hospital room. YOYO *in a dressing gown, in a chair. Also his* MOTHER, *a Greek woman dressed in black, a Russian Orthodox* PRIEST *and* CATHERINE.

PRIEST: (*Scatters incense over* YOYO *and his* MOTHER) Almighty master, put away from your servant Giorgos the spirit of disease and every malady, every wound, every fever and every seizure. And if he has sins or transgressions, loose, remit and forgive them for the sake of your love towards mankind. (*He sprinkles* YOYO *with water.* BIDDY *comes in.*)

YOYO: (*Weakly*) I didn't expect you so soon . . .

BIDDY: I was at a gallery.

YOYO: This is my mother. Mama, my wife.

YOYO'S MOTHER: (*In a heavy Greek accent*) Ah, you have a lovely wife and a beautiful mistress, you have done very well, Giorgos.

(BIDDY *stares at* CATHERINE.)

This one look English, but the other one is younger.

(*The* PRIEST *continues praying.*)

My son: he has become such a gentleman.

(CATHERINE *goes to* BIDDY.)

CATHERINE: I thought you knew. I am sorry.

BIDDY: Please!

(*She brushes her away.* CATHERINE *kisses the* PRIEST's *hand and* YOYO, *and leaves.*)

YOYO: Biddy, please, come close.

(*She doesn't.*)

I am sorry: Katerina, three years, so . . . I have to tell you, one of the houses has to be sold.

YOYO'S MOTHER: 'He who has two wives loses his heart, but he who has two houses loses his head . . .'

YOYO: The banks . . . There's some good news. I've been asked on a committee at the Progress, the Roof Committee, it's the most prestigious. It's because of the paintings. Thank you. Mama has the letter.

YOYO'S MOTHER: Beautiful letter, beautiful. The ink.

(*The* PRIEST *comes next to her.*)

PRIEST: If he dies and you are angry with him, you will feel tormented for the rest of your life.

BIDDY: He's not going to die. The doctor said the kidney was taking . . . it's a temporary rejection.

PRIEST: I knew a man once who had left his girlfriend after a furious argument. She was killed suddenly. He spent twenty years trying to find peace. That is what it means to be haunted.

BIDDY: He has a mistress.

PRIEST: That was foolish.

BIDDY: I suppose she's more interesting than I am.

PRIEST: You will be interesting if you forgive him.

BIDDY: I don't know what forgiveness means.

PRIEST: It is accepting the weight of another's pain, which, measured against your own, is found greater. Even if you have to cheat at the scales.

BIDDY: His mother . . . he was never in touch with her.

PRIEST: She is letting him go in peace.

YOYO'S MOTHER: Giorgi, sing, you have such a beautiful voice. I remember it so well. Sing.

BIDDY: He never sings.

PRIEST: I've noticed that people who deny their childhood often lose their voices . . .

YOYO'S MOTHER: Where is your mistress, has she gone? Does she know what a beautiful voice you have, Giorgi?

PRIEST: At the Orthodox funeral service . . .

BIDDY: He's not going to die.

PRIEST: We stand with lit candles. This is to say that this person has brought at least a flicker of light into the world and that we will keep this light and set out to be the continuation of what was good and true in this person – who will then not have lived in vain.

YOYO: (*To* BIDDY) I miss Greece . . . I'll take you there, would you like that? I am not sure England is what I thought it was, and I have made fussy buildings . . . a lie. Biddy, do you understand?

BIDDY: Yes . . .

YOYO: Thank you. You'll continue the collection . . .

BIDDY: Why a Russian priest?

YOYO: They're more . . . well, better class. *Emigrés*.

YOYO'S MOTHER: Sing, Giorgi, sing. I'll sing with you. We'll sing something Greek.

(YOYO *and* YOYO'S MOTHER *sing*.)

SCENE TWENTY-ONE: FIONA; SELF-PORTRAIT

JEAN *sits, taking notes*.

FIONA: I've always felt sorry for the Ugly Sisters. In some

versions, their mother tells them to cut off a part of their foot to get it into the slipper. It works and they go off with the Prince until he notices blood. No fine Prince wants to see a lot of blood, so he takes them back and eventually gets the diaphanous Cinderella, who will not bleed. Great, but what happens to the sisters with their half foot? How do they spend the rest of their lives? Are they angry with their mother for telling them to cut off part of their foot? Or do they just get on with it?

I am living alone in a big house with a great big studio. Julia gave me a lot of money to start out with, to get me to leave Jeremy. It was stupid of her because there isn't much money about and art isn't selling very well.

And so I pace about and paint. I work very hard. I am not happy but I don't think I ever expected that. I wake early every morning. Some days the world is at war, some days that doesn't matter. Sometimes I paint the darkness of it all, sometimes I paint light. Sometimes I paint laughter.

I know you, you're waiting for the sentence that is going to click it all into place. I don't have it. This is the nineties, Jean. I'm not going to pretend to have it.

SCENE TWENTY-TWO: BIDDY IN THE LANDSCAPE

BIDDY *posing*, STEPHEN *painting her*.

BIDDY: I like posing. I think of so many things. I remember my last year at Benenden, noticing beautiful things. The spring, the countryside of Kent, the oasts, the tennis teacher. I felt almost drunk on it all . . . it was like a Constable. And then, then, I stopped looking. That first marriage, now I see it was well, minimalist, a Lewitt, or possibly a Carl André.

Then Yoyo. That was a kind of Schnabel, a mess. Because we were always stuffing ourselves: houses, cars, a yacht, then art. Now it's fashionable to be sober and lead a quiet life, looking for a forgotten meaning, depth. How long will that last? In ten years' time will we be talking about the virtues of the new greed?

69

STEPHEN: Don't move. When England began doubting itself, why did it have to stop loving itself?

BIDDY: Are you enjoying being famous again?

STEPHEN: I don't think Julia's gallery is going to last. The art market may be terminally ill.

BIDDY: It could reject you and die, like Yoyo.

STEPHEN: No one trusts anybody's opinion. I'm waiting to meet someone who feels certain about something, anything. But yes, I'm enjoying not being angry.

BIDDY: I've been asked to give a lecture on England and the new art. Me. I've become interesting. It's what Yoyo wanted . . . Yoyo. I wonder if someone told him it was a Turkish kidney or if his body just knew.

I'm going to have to charge a high price for that lecture. All that wealth: vanished. And I won't sell the paintings. I'm lucky to have a flat. He bought it for that mistress of his, you know, but luckily it was in his name and there was no will. Well, there was a piece of paper, but I got rid of that, it wasn't legal anyway. She could have gone to a good lawyer and claimed to be a kept mistress, she could have got something, apparently the law is very generous to kept mistresses. She must have been stupid or maybe she was proud. I didn't even let her know when the funeral was. You can't have two widows wandering around, it looks silly. And grief makes you cruel. I'm sorry now.
(*Pause.*)
I was always afraid of being alone. And now it's happened. It isn't so bad.
(STEPHEN *goes to rearrange some drapery on* BIDDY.)
It's rather good, my body . . .

STEPHEN: When I started this painting, there were three birds and you were a vanishing figure, but you've taken over the canvas.
(*He puts his hands on her breasts.*)

BIDDY: When you do that, Stephen, I think: I am happy in a most ordinary way, happy to be painted among the daffodils. I am happy to be loved today, that's all I want. I don't want more.

70

STEPHEN: Not daffodils. Foxgloves, fireweed and a wood
anemone. And then, only a shape, a colour.
(STEPHEN *goes back to work. Fade.*)